Mandala Coloring Book

Stress Relieving Patterns

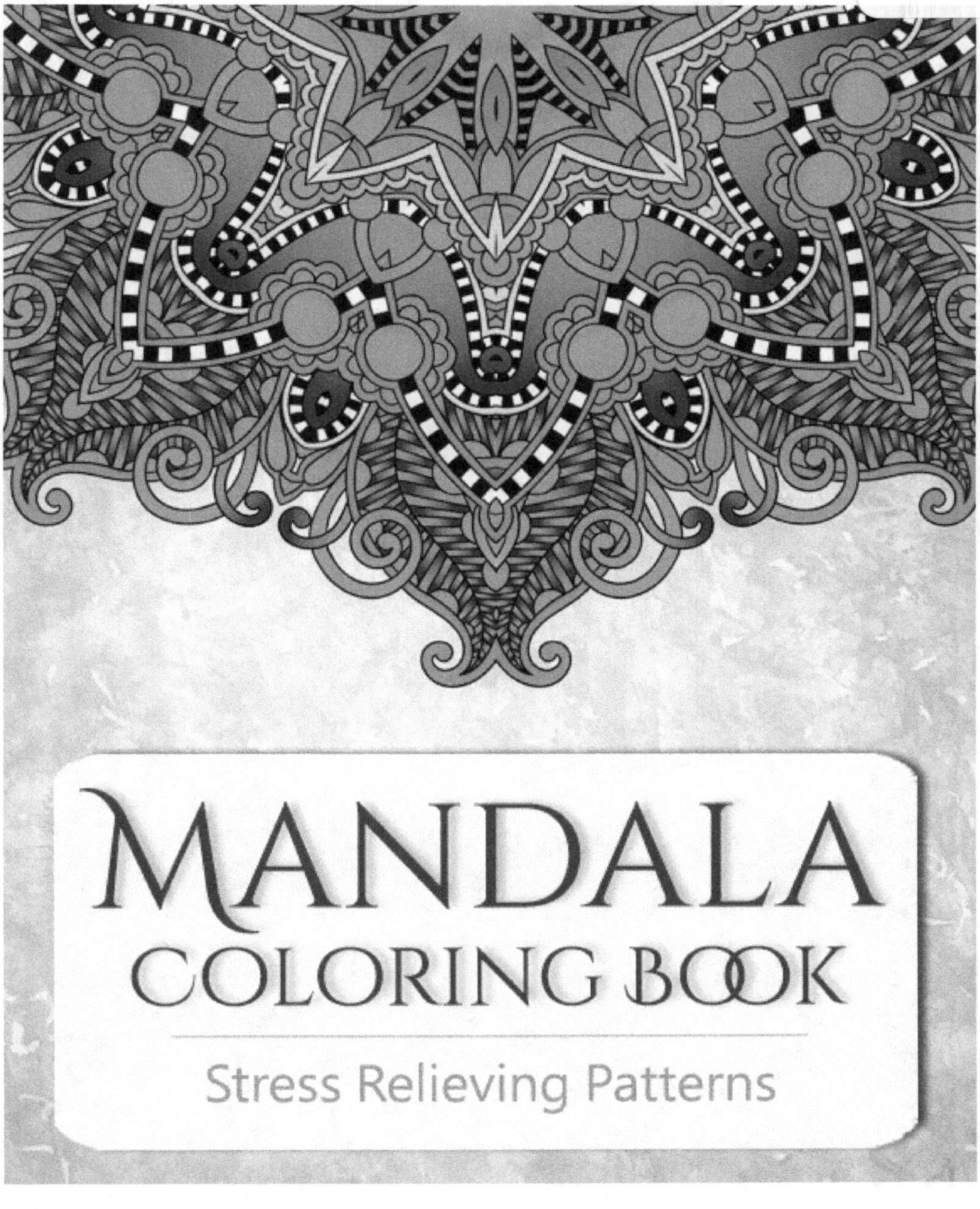

Vol. 20

V ART™

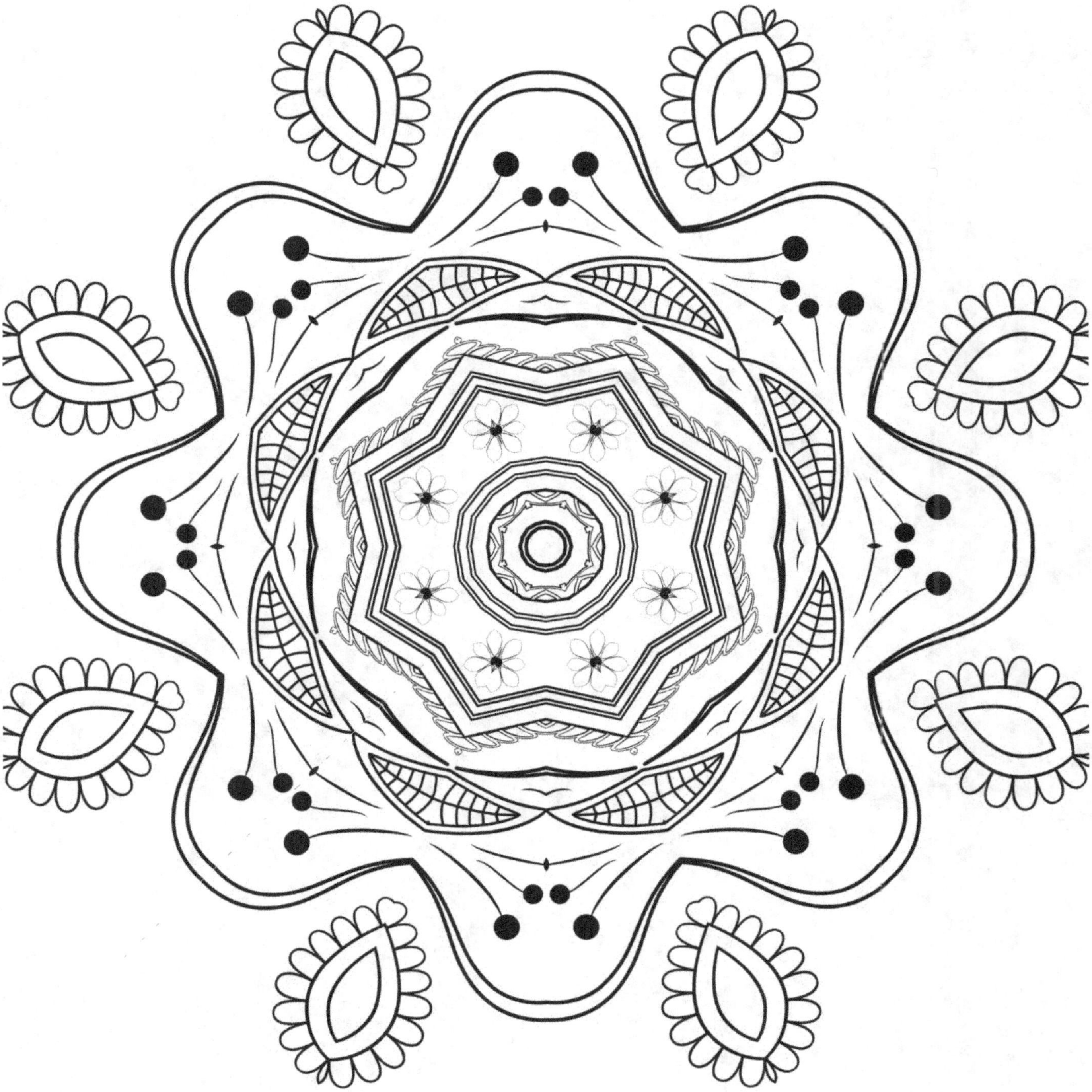

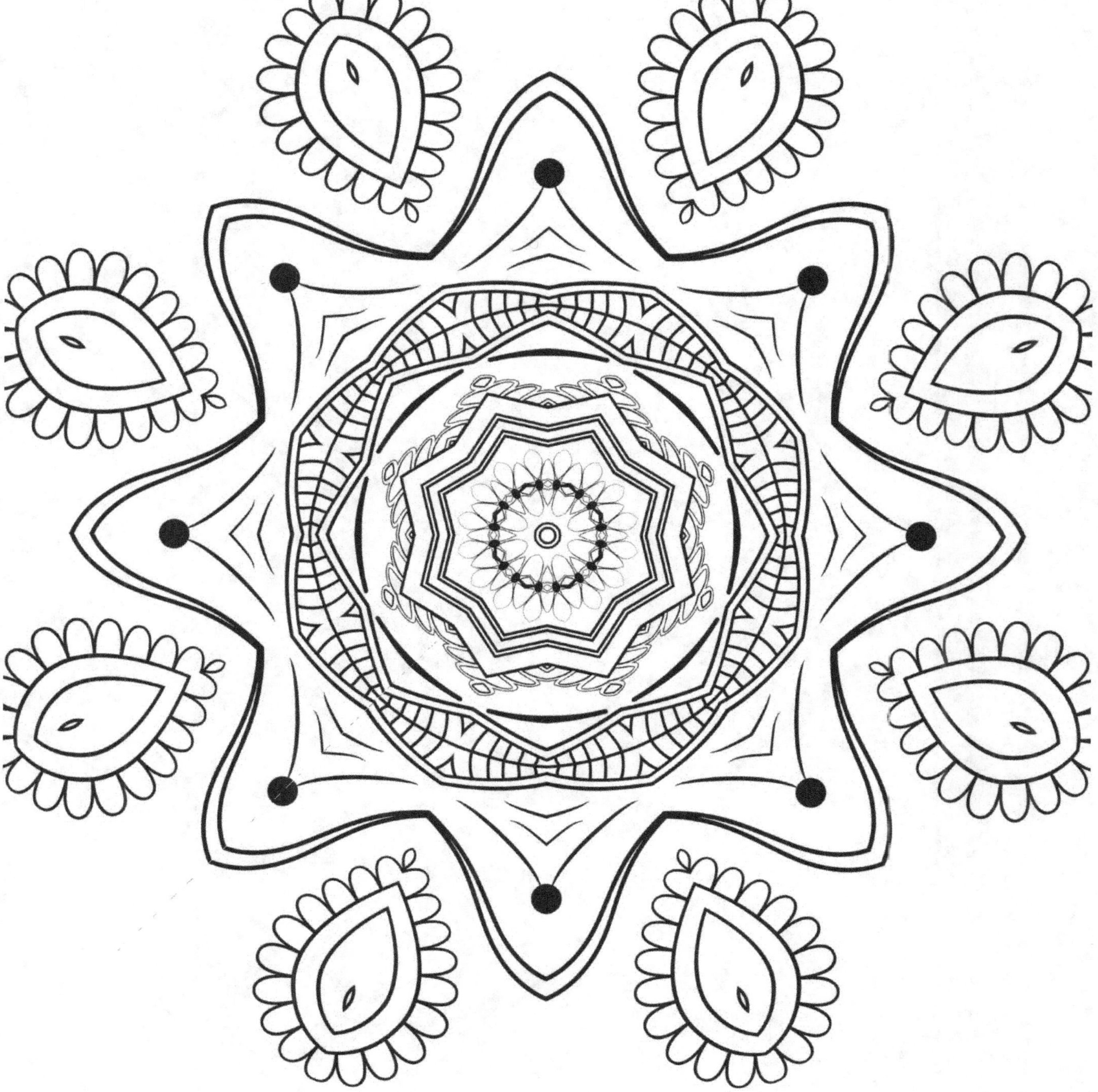

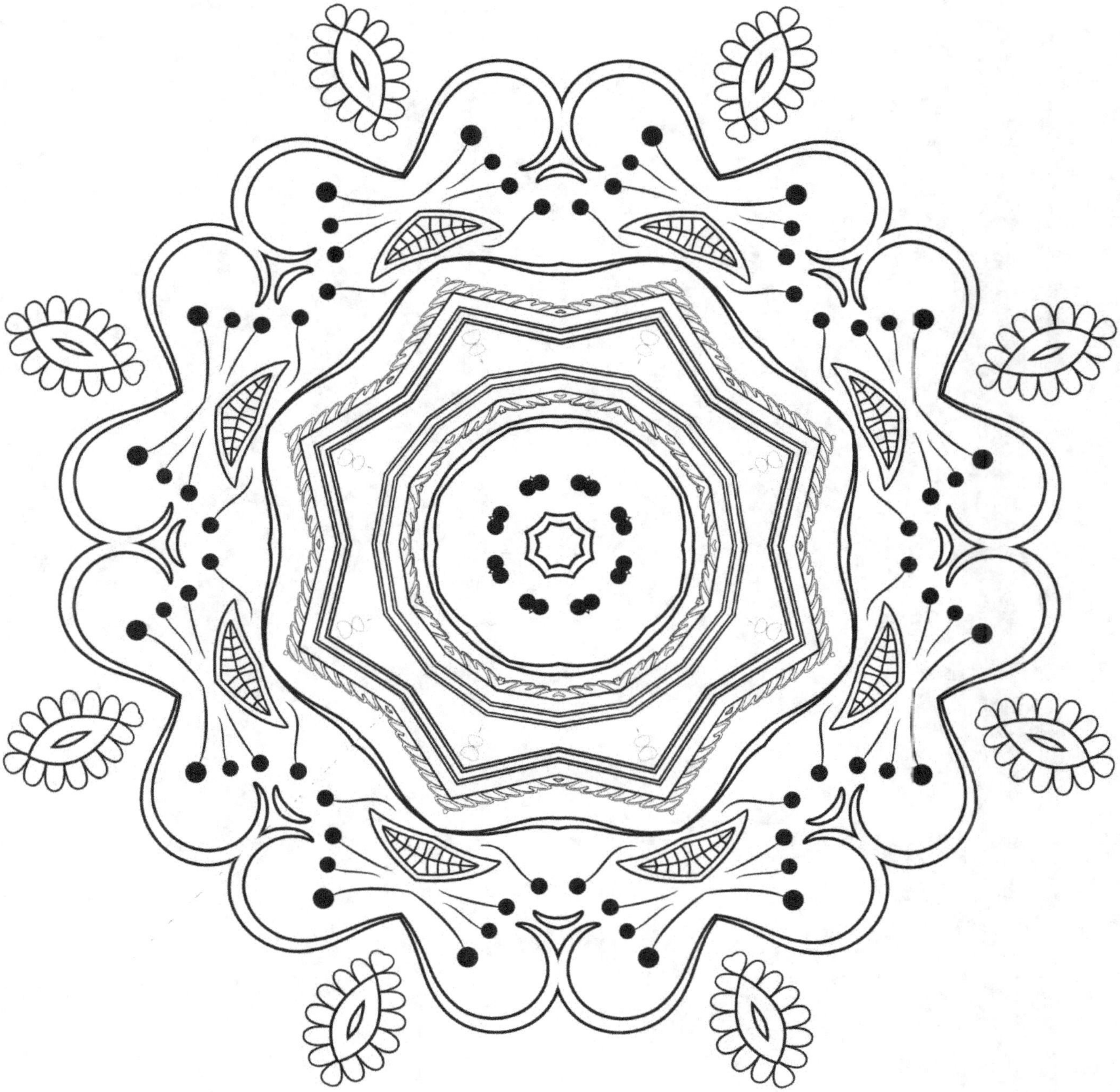

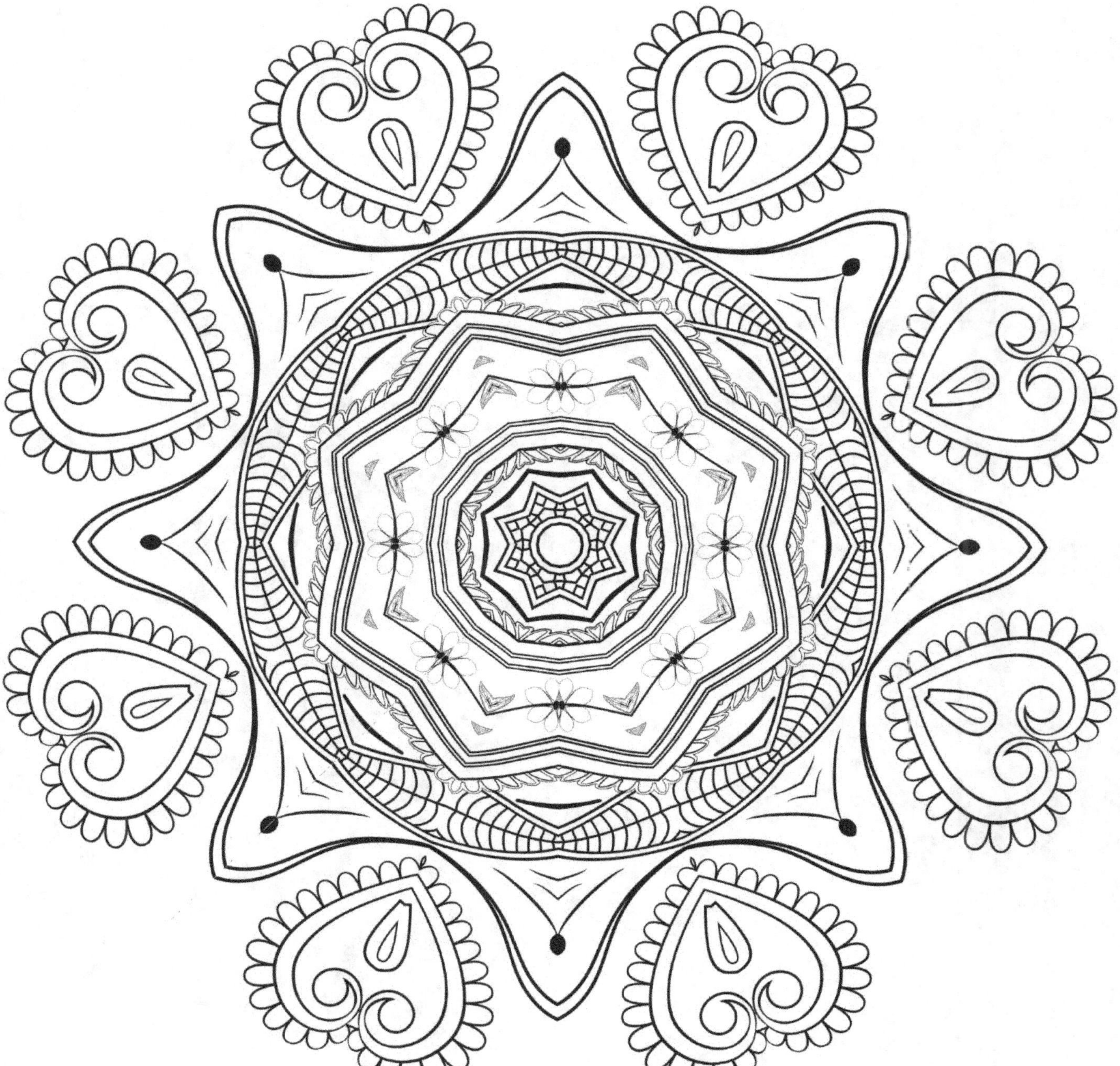

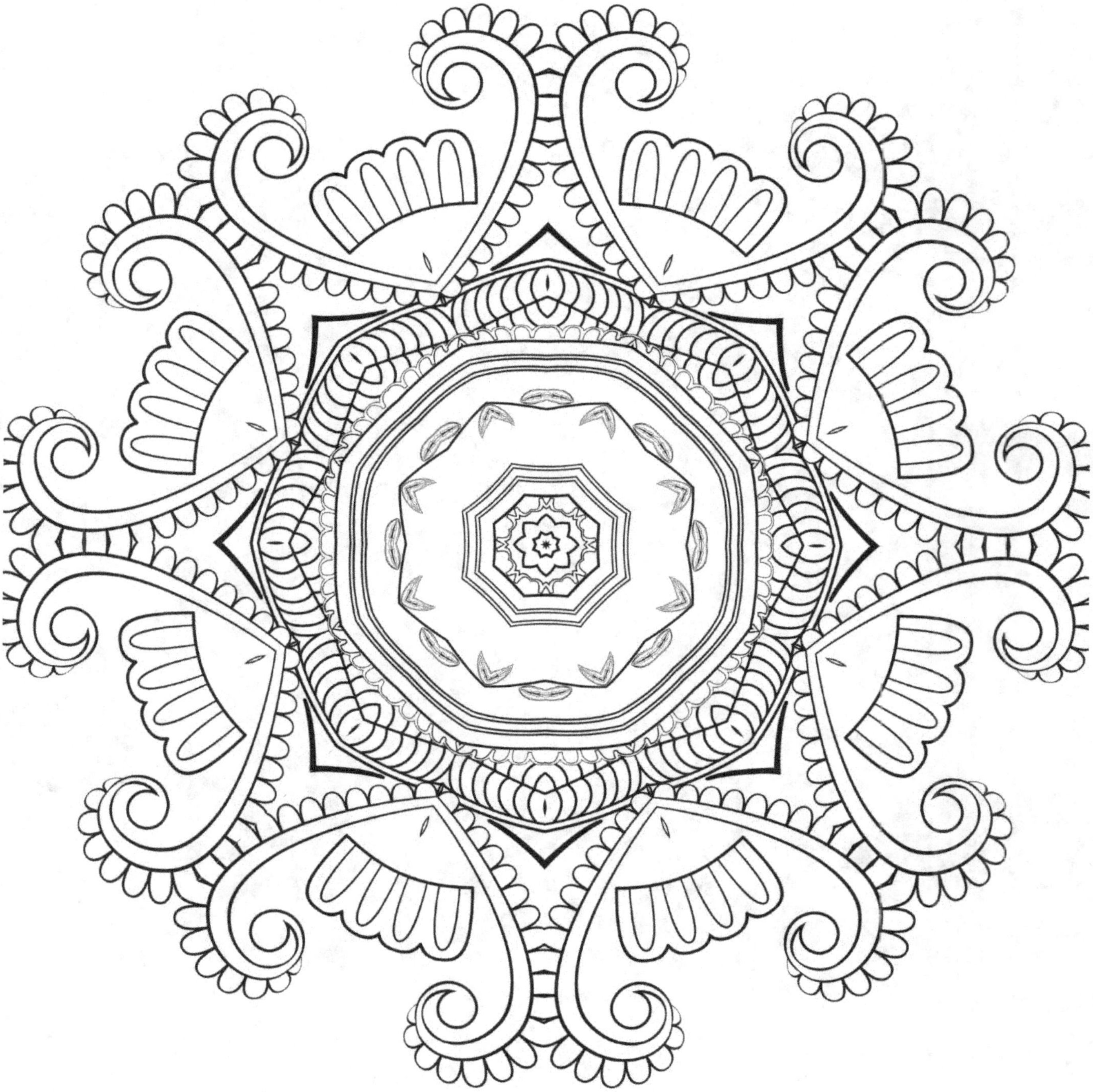

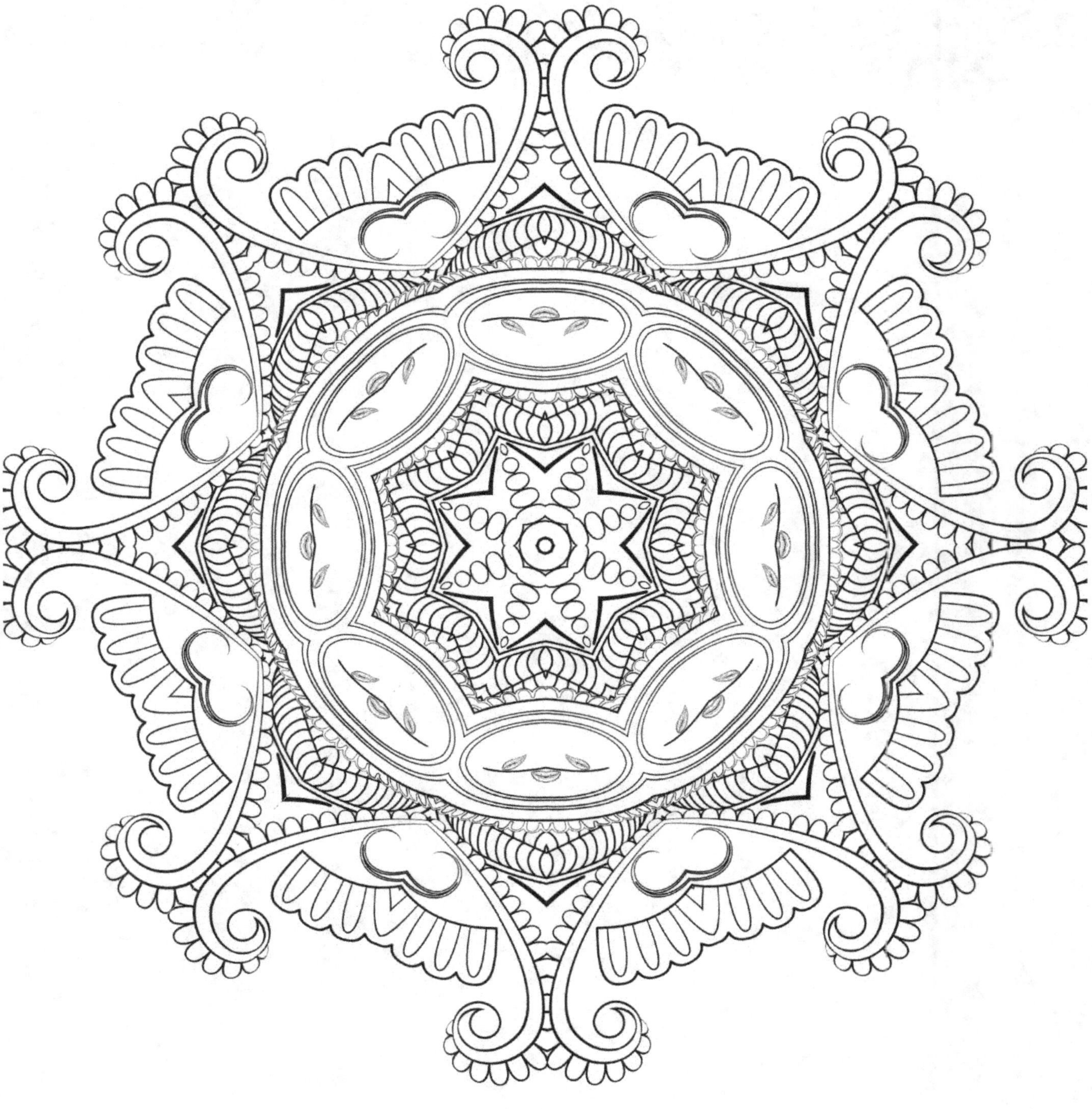

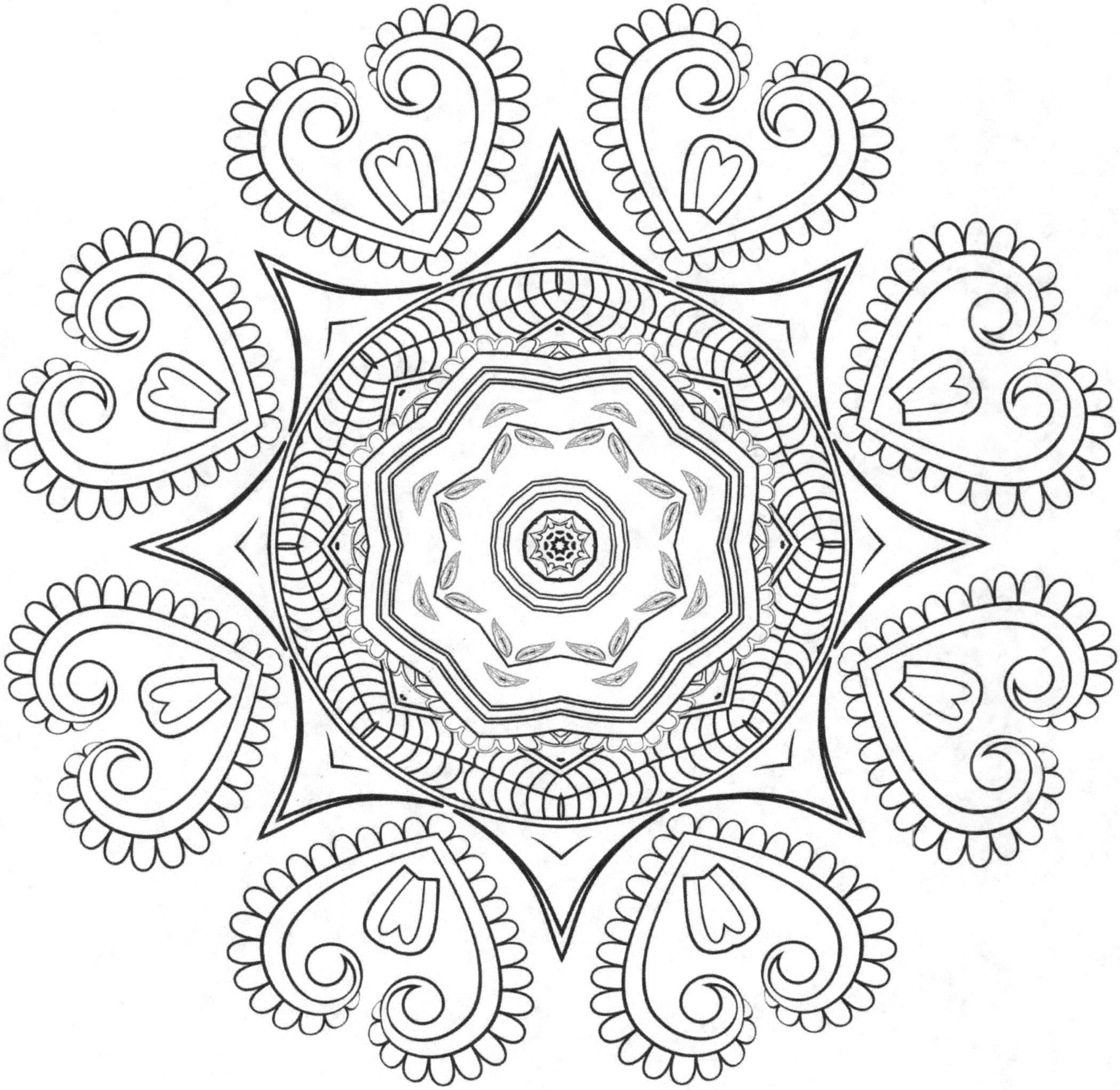

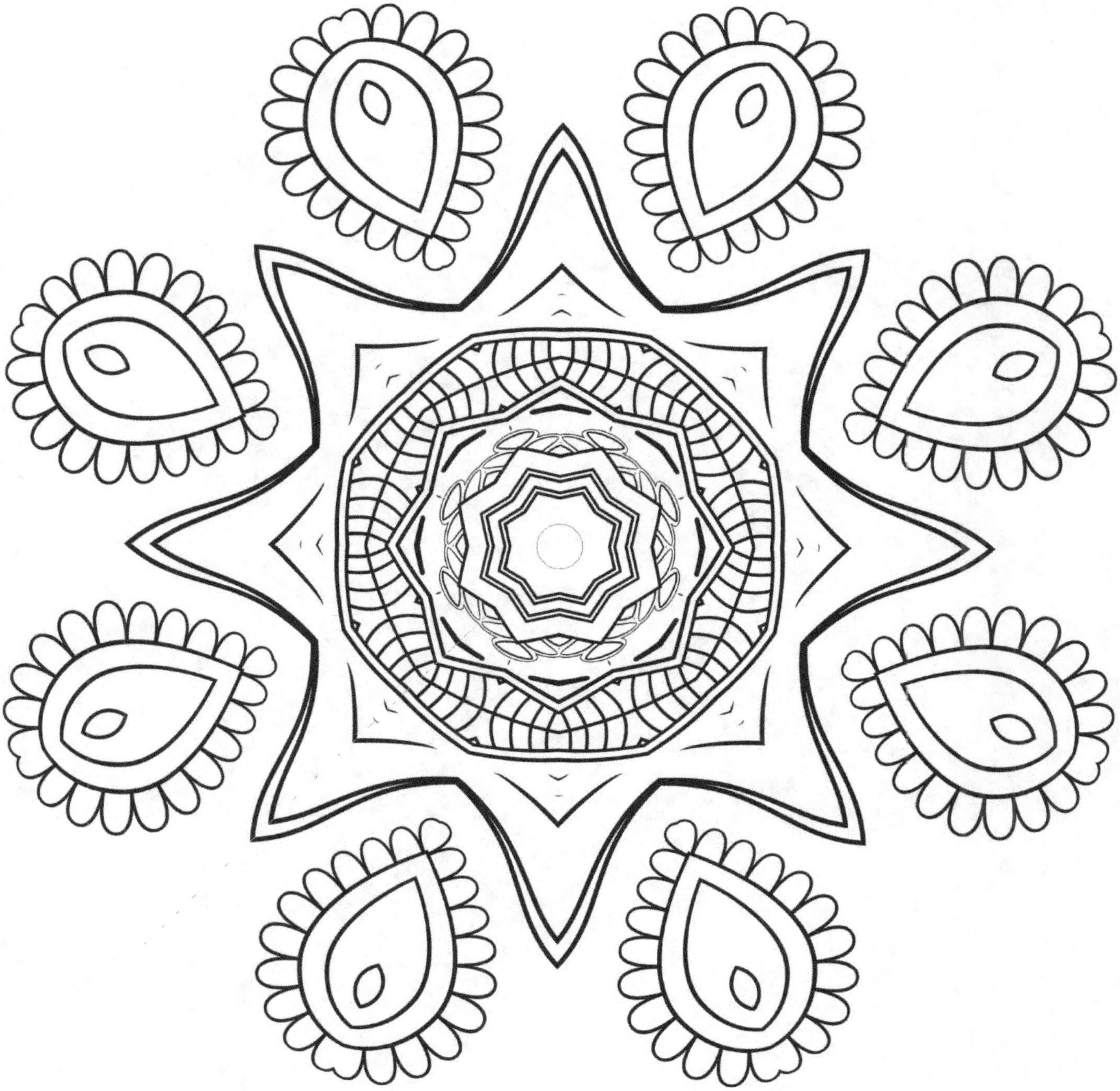

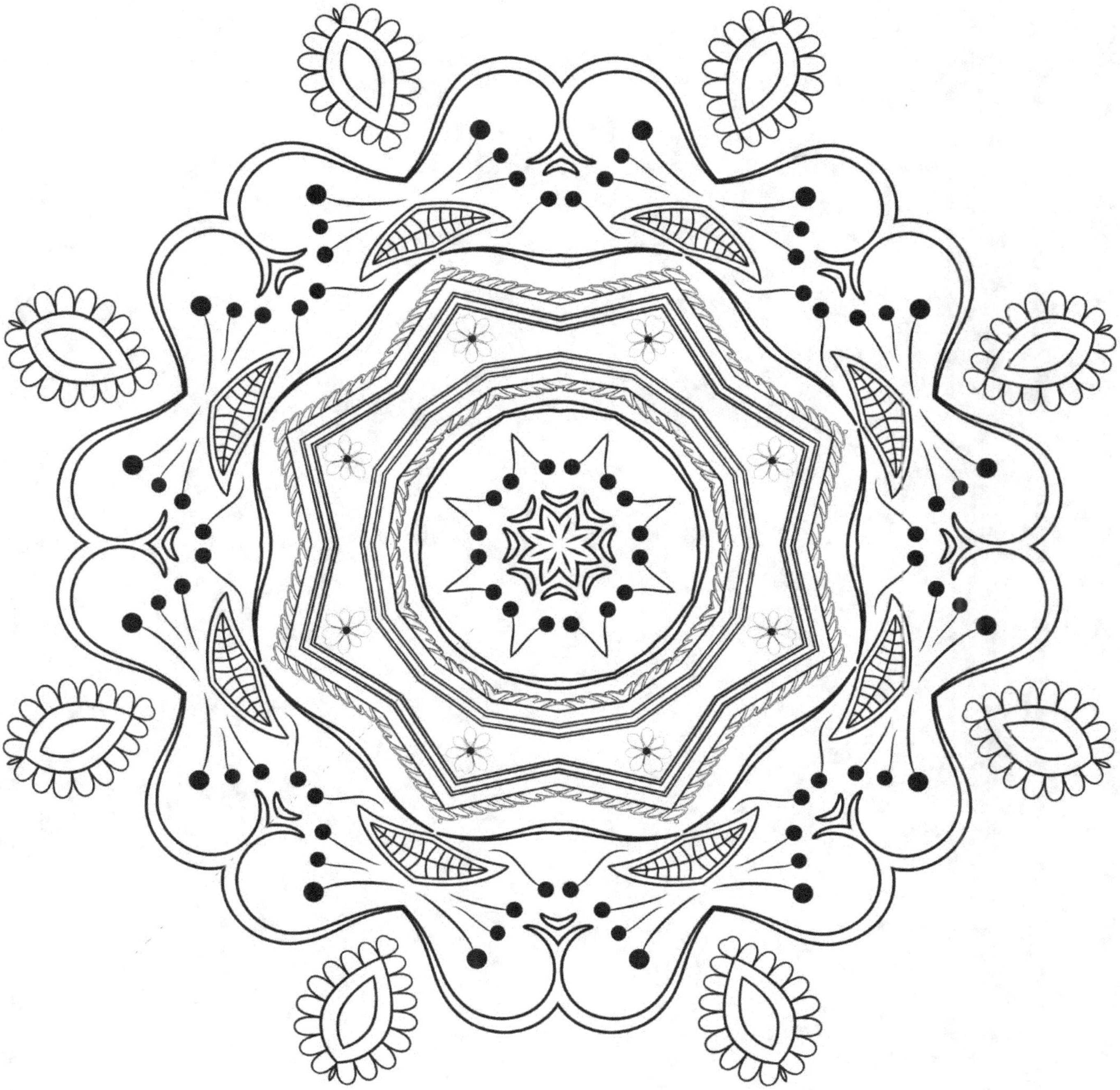

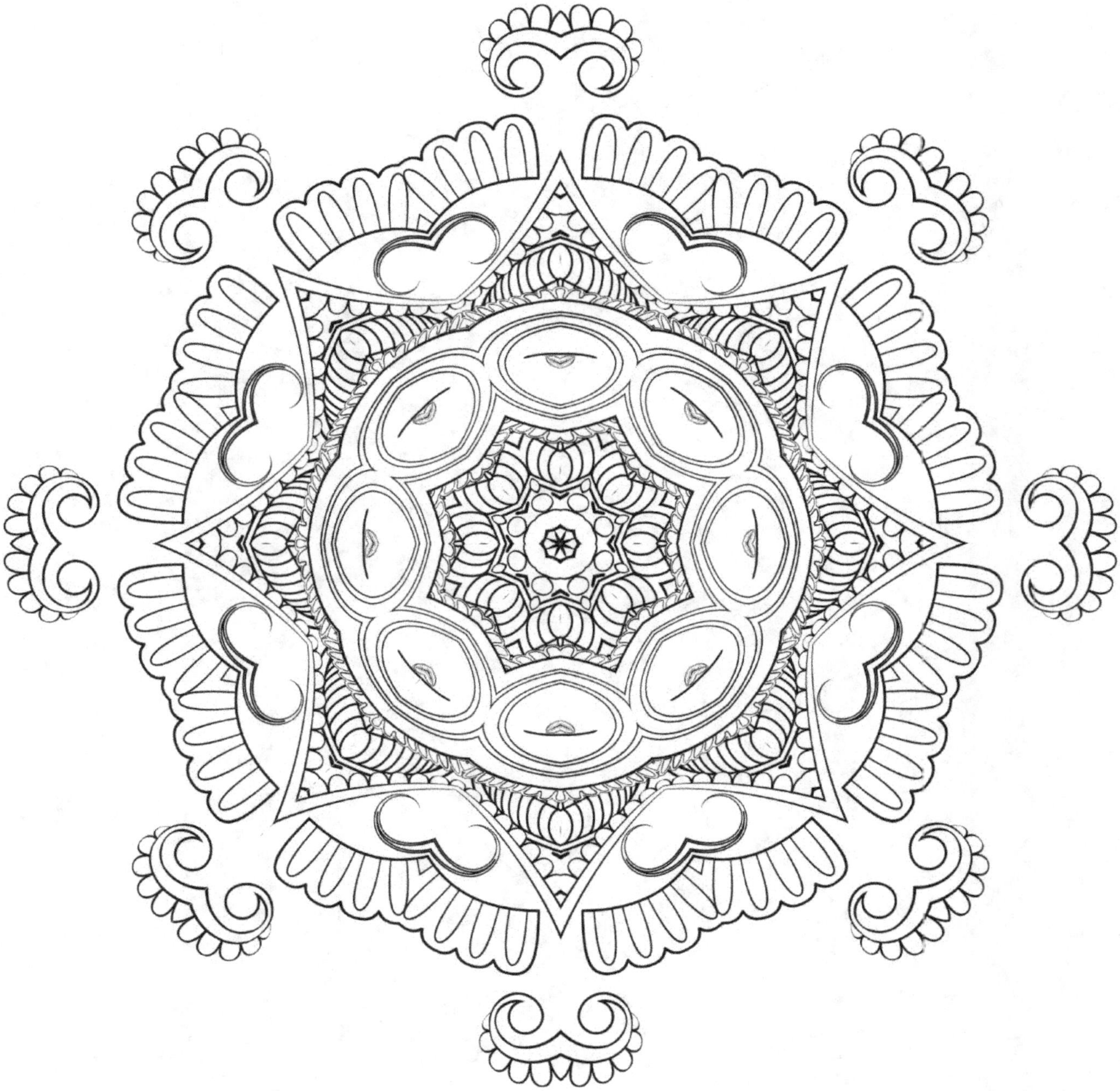

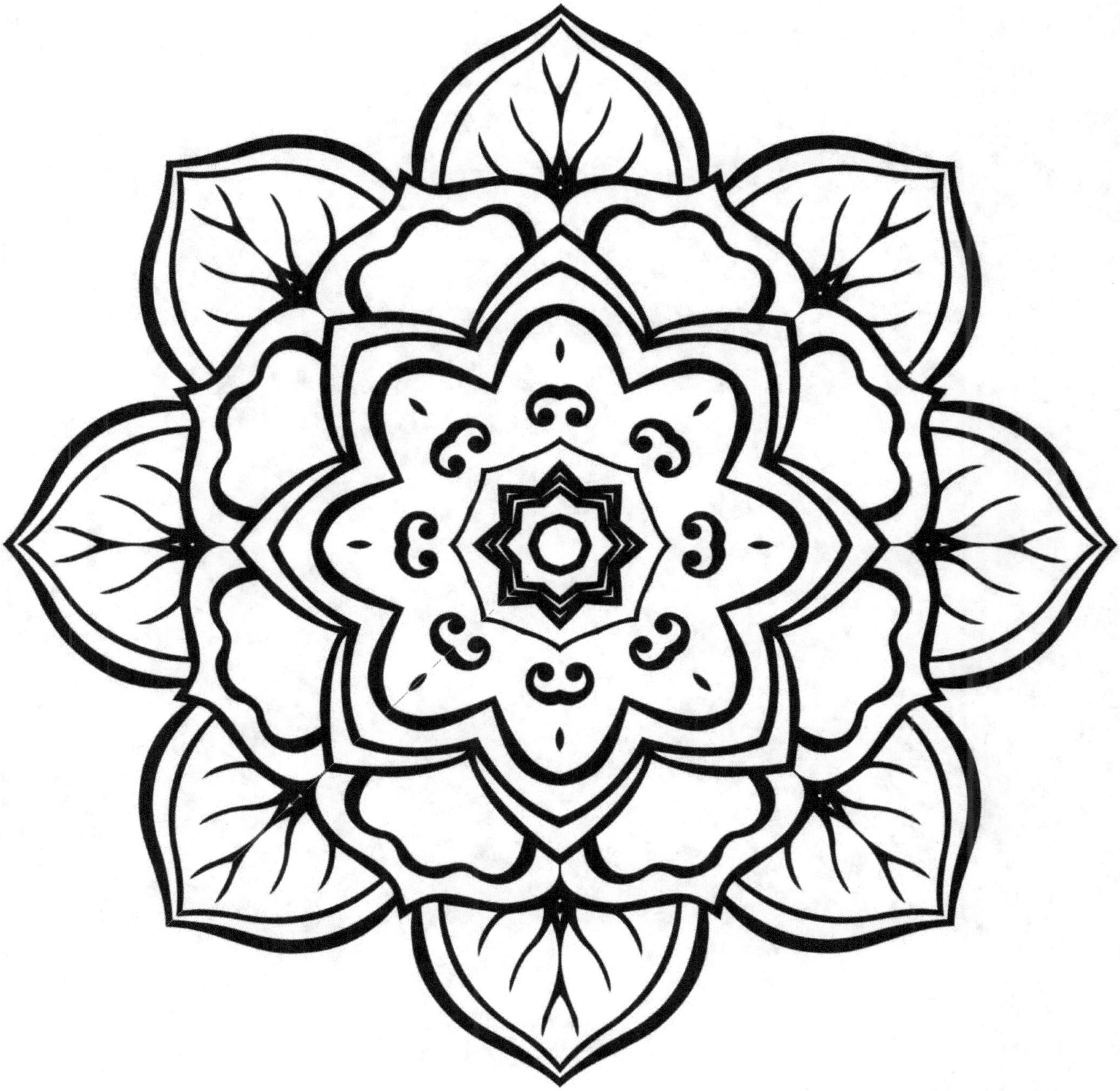

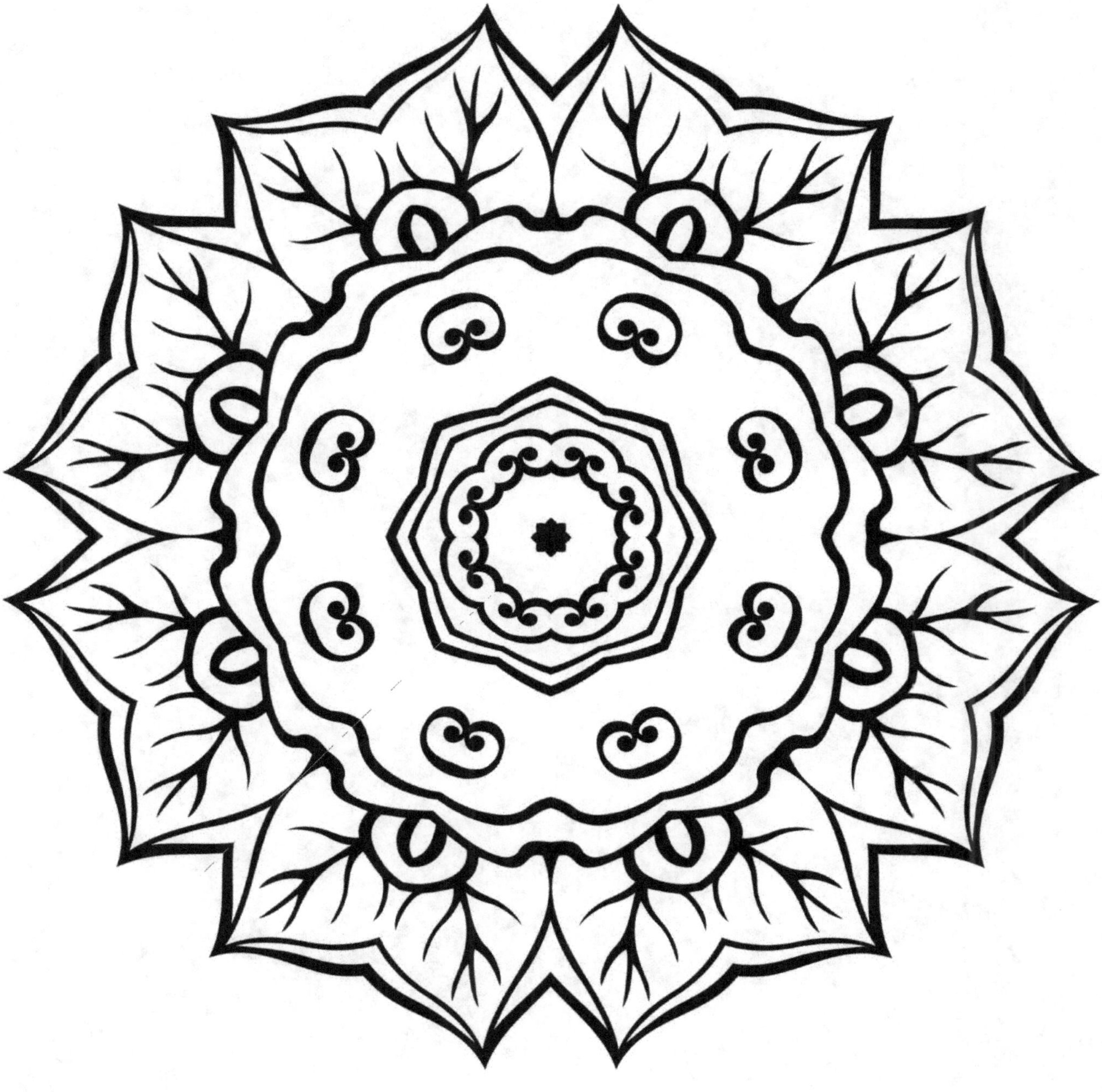

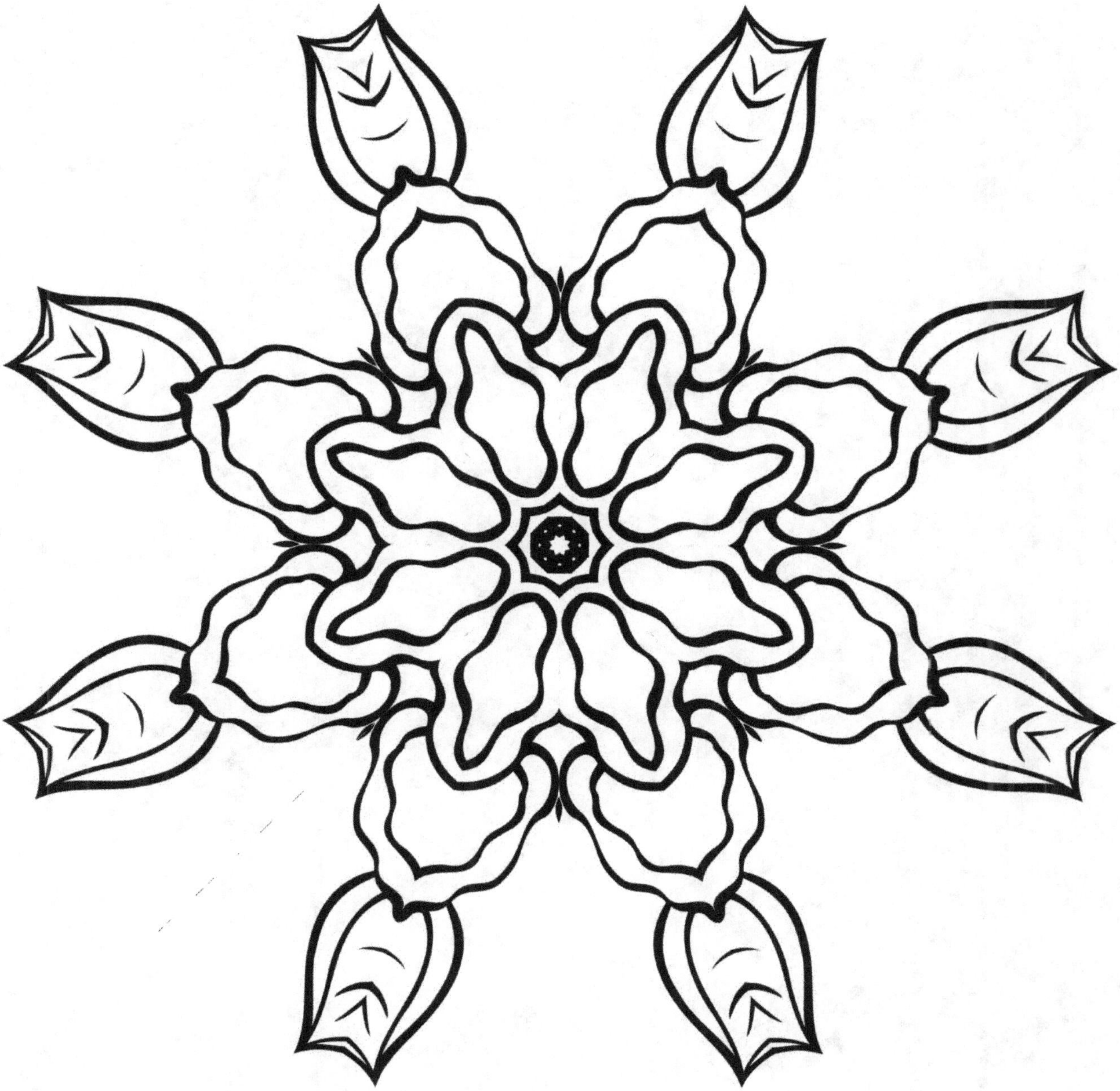

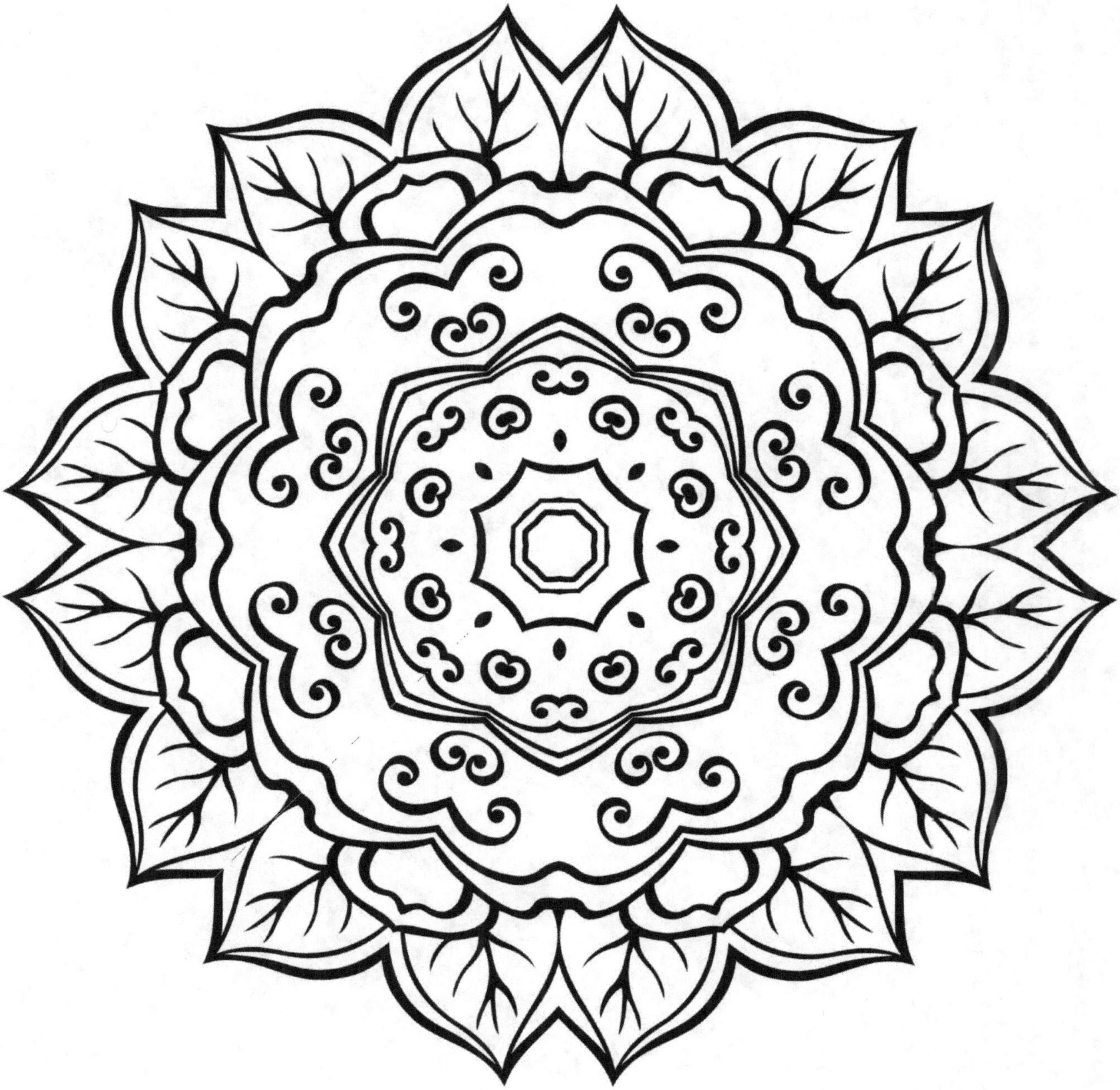

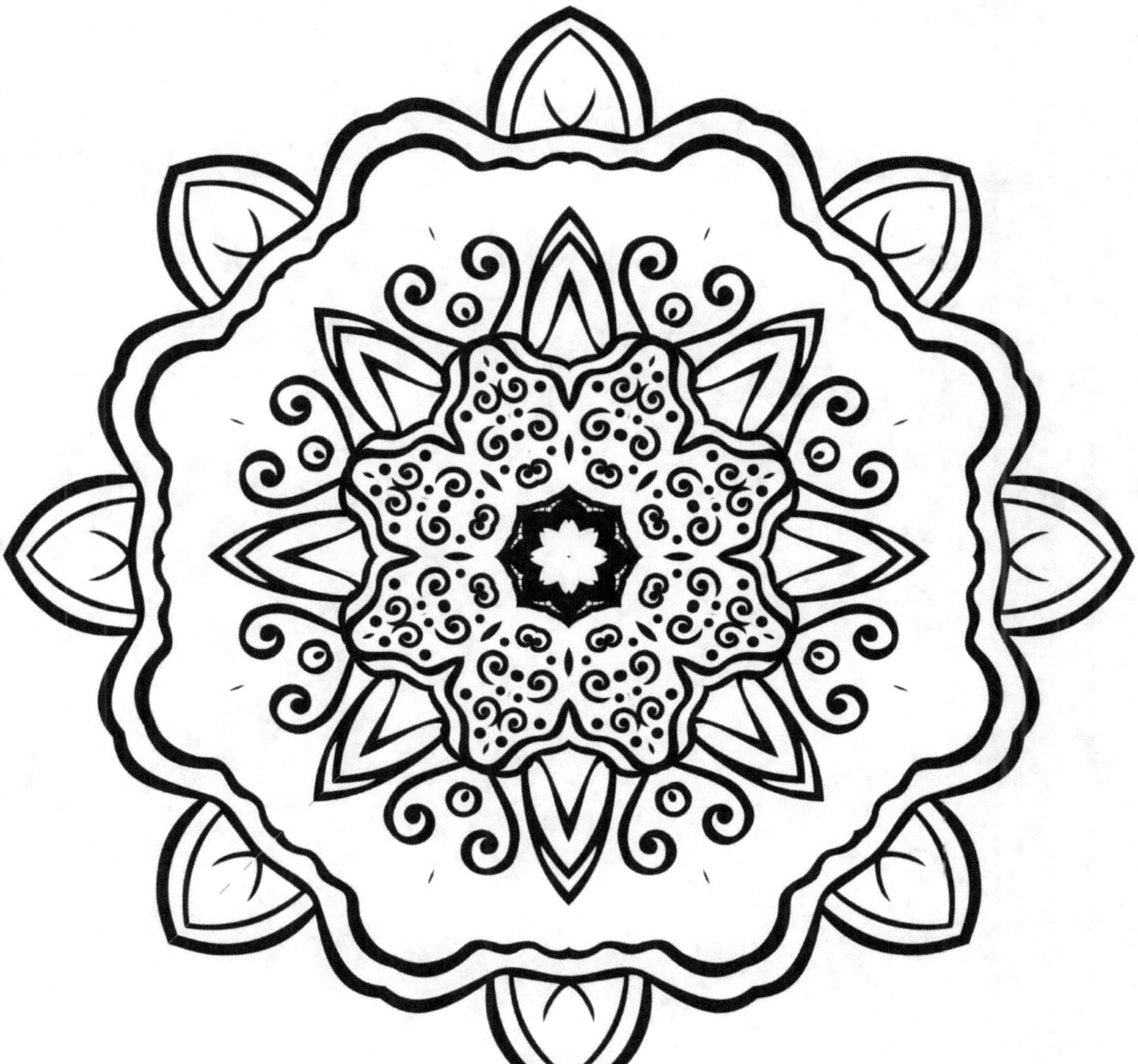

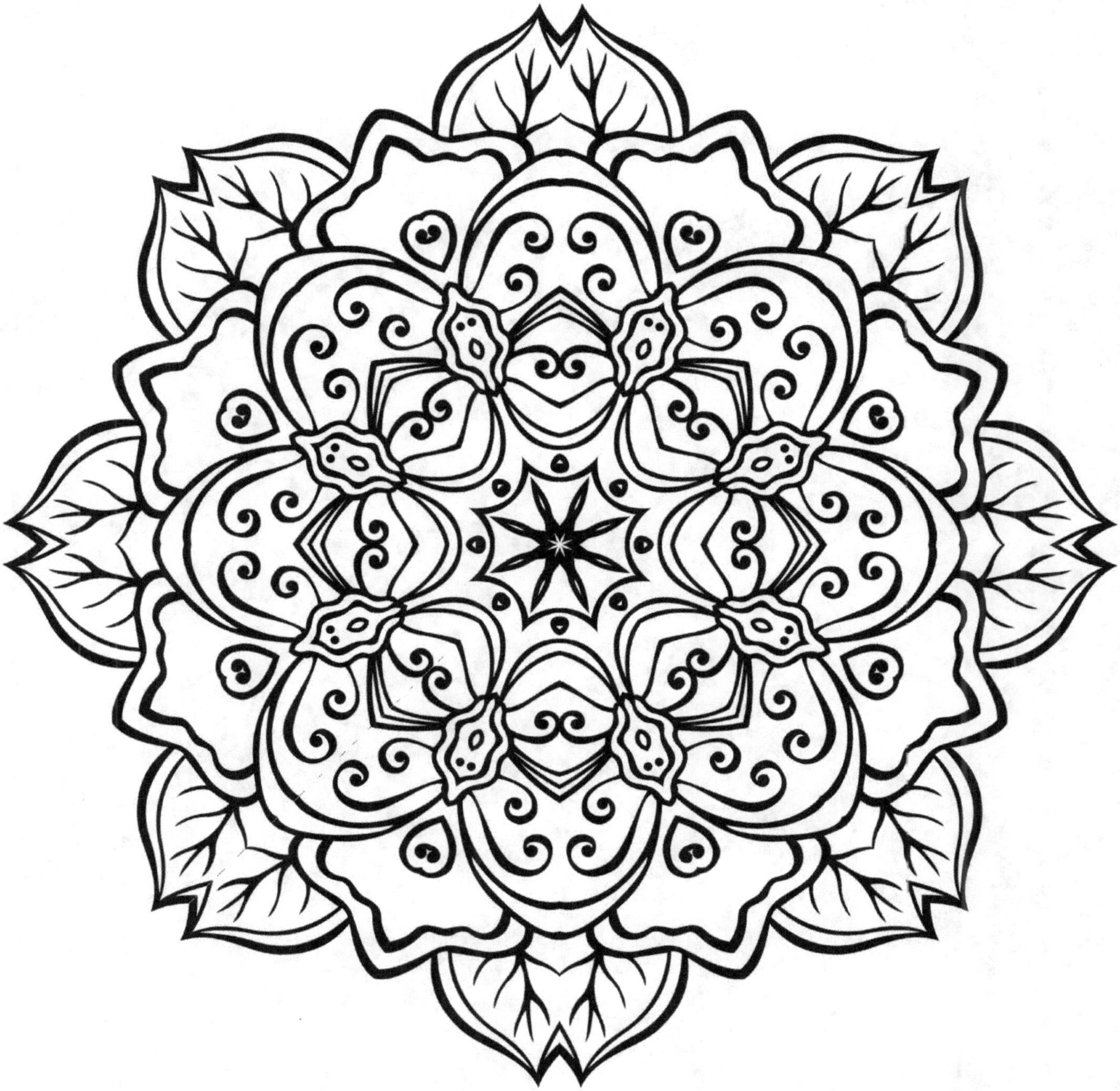

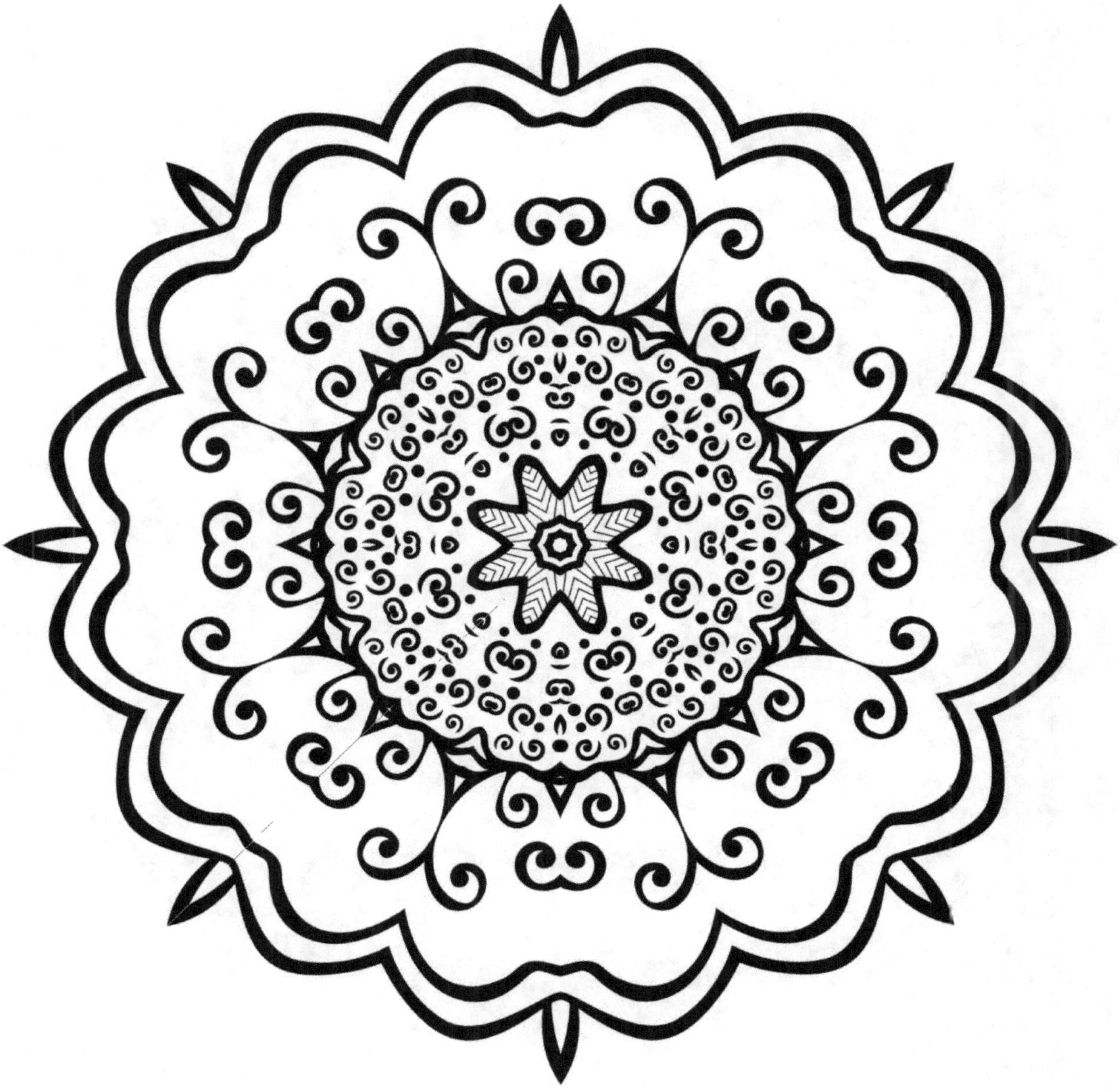

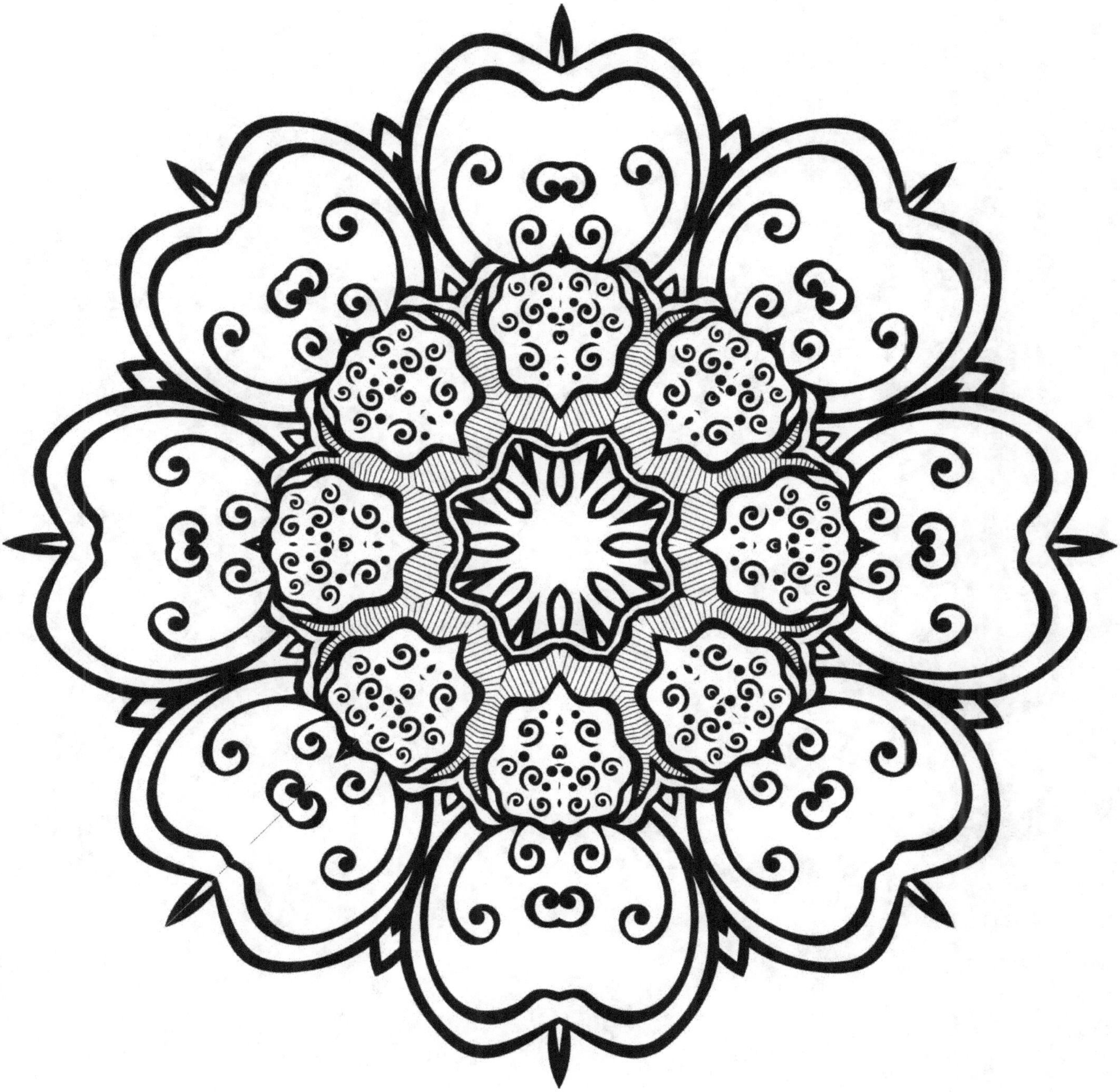

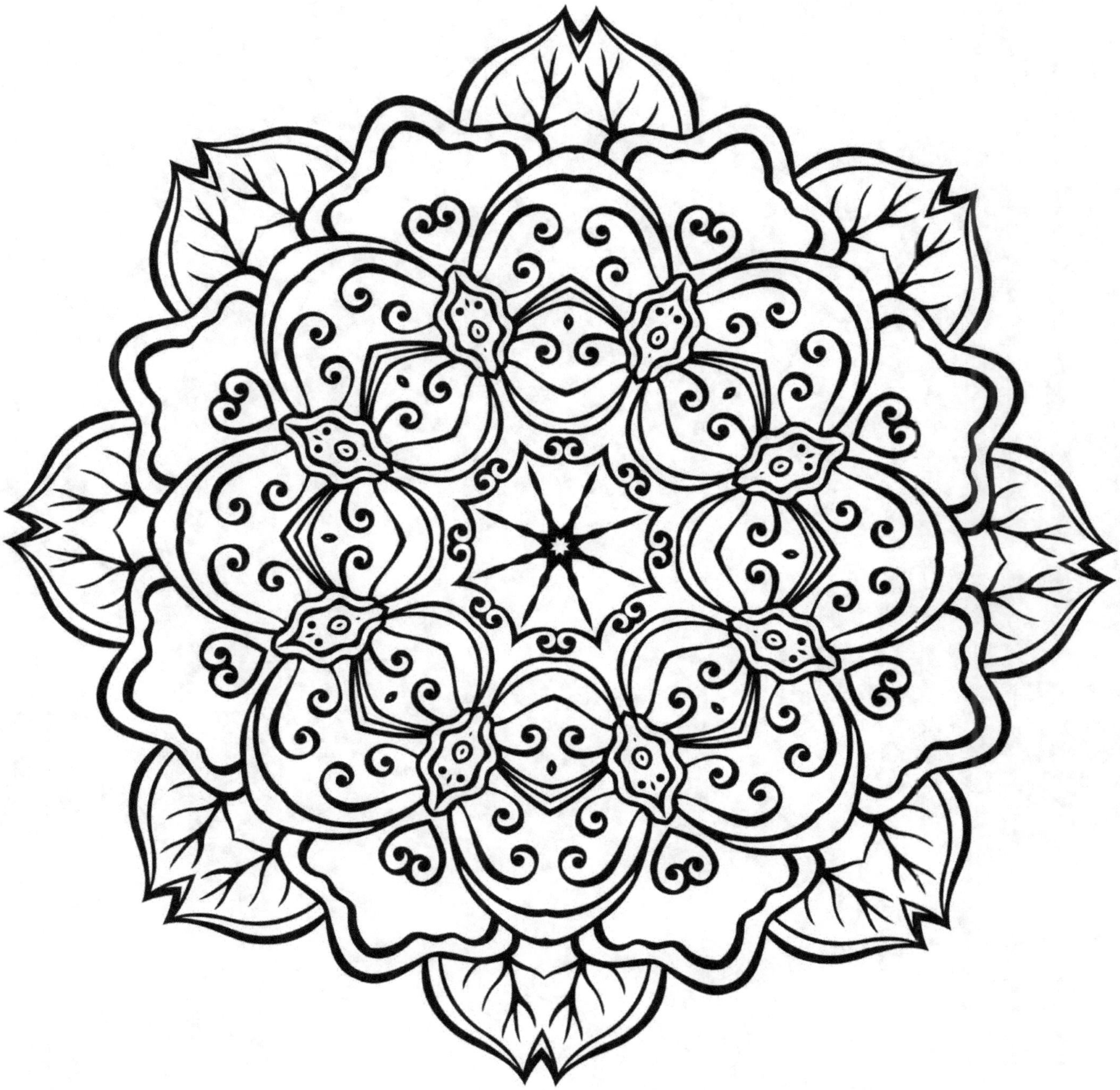

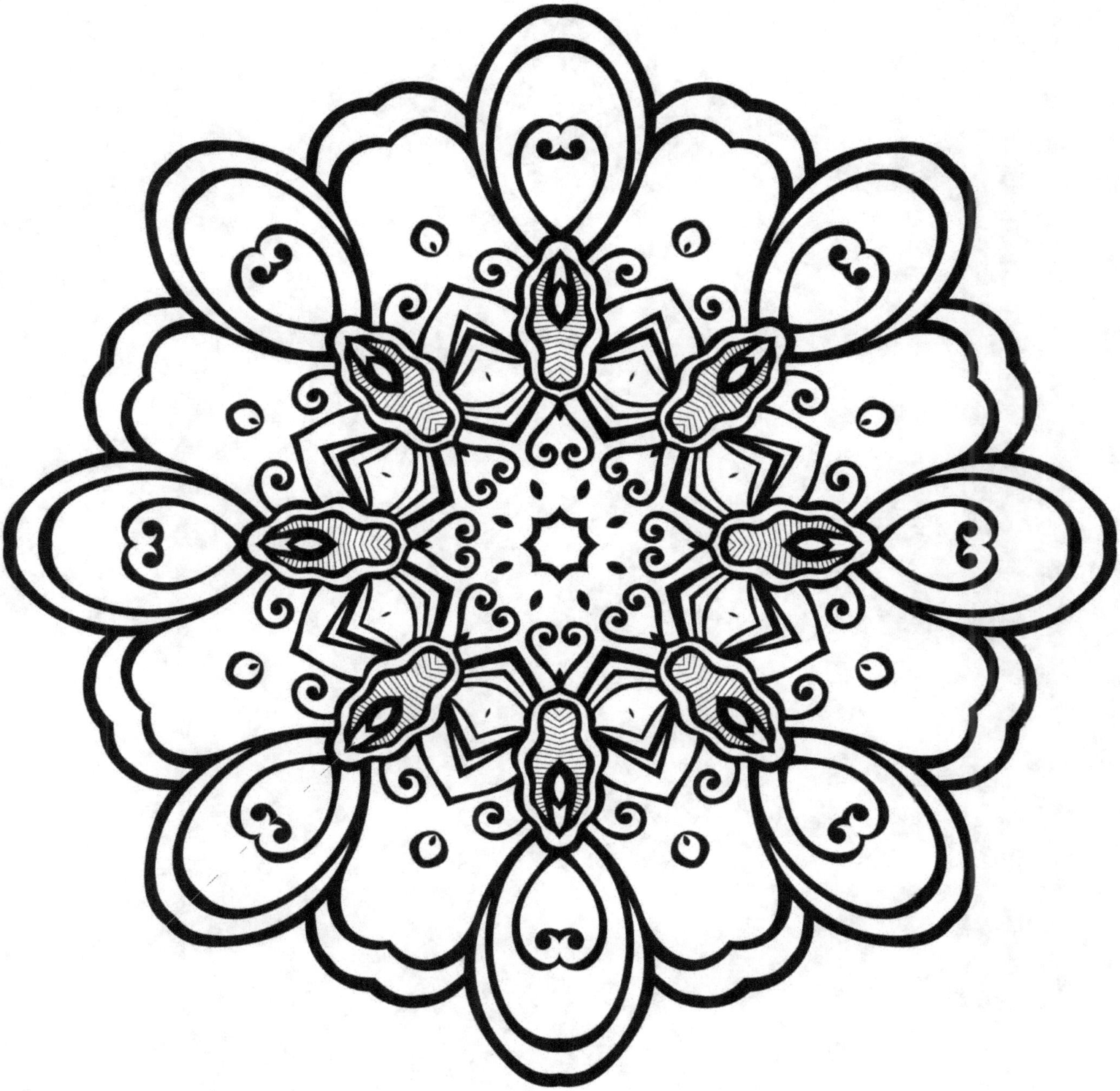

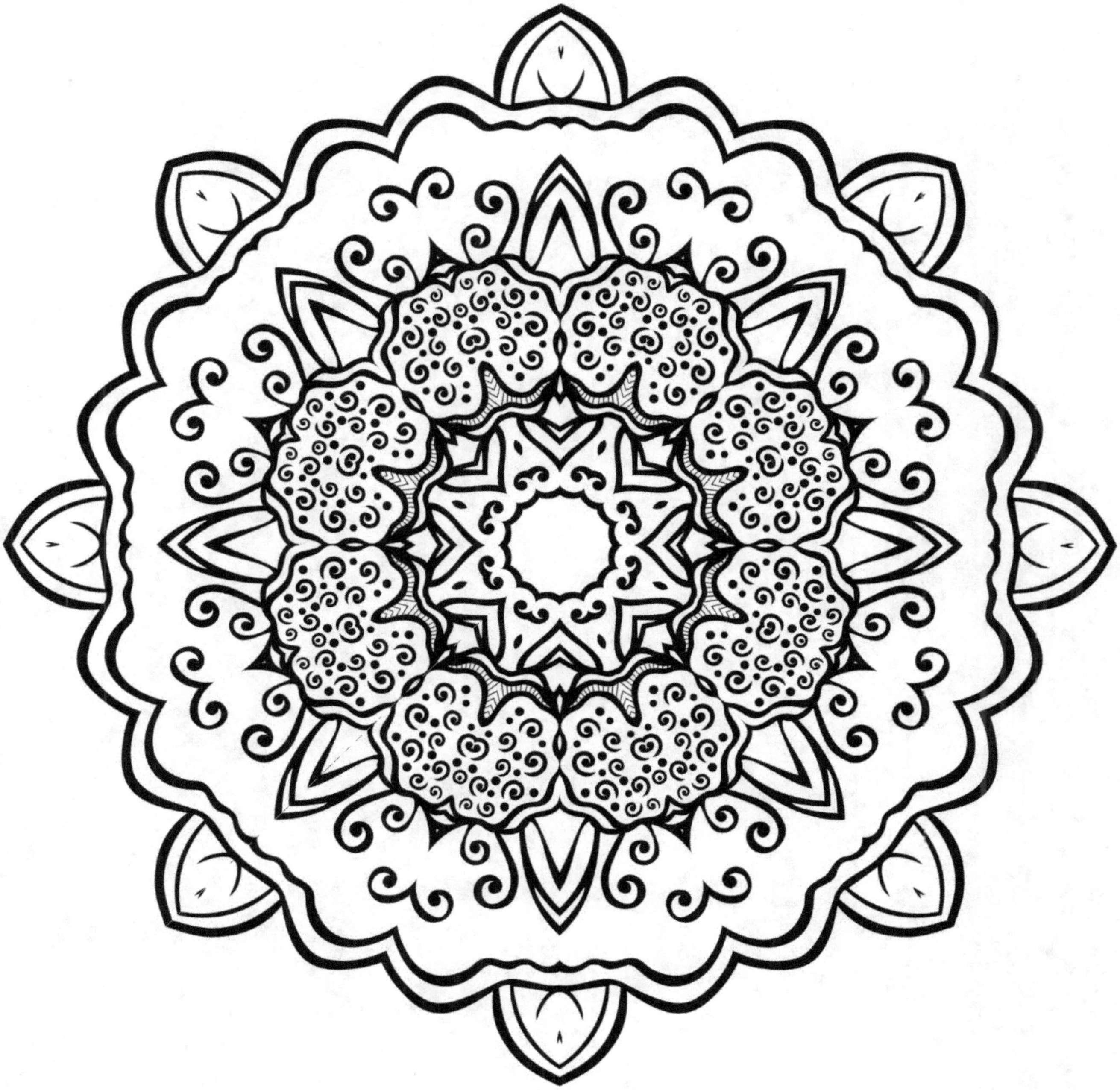

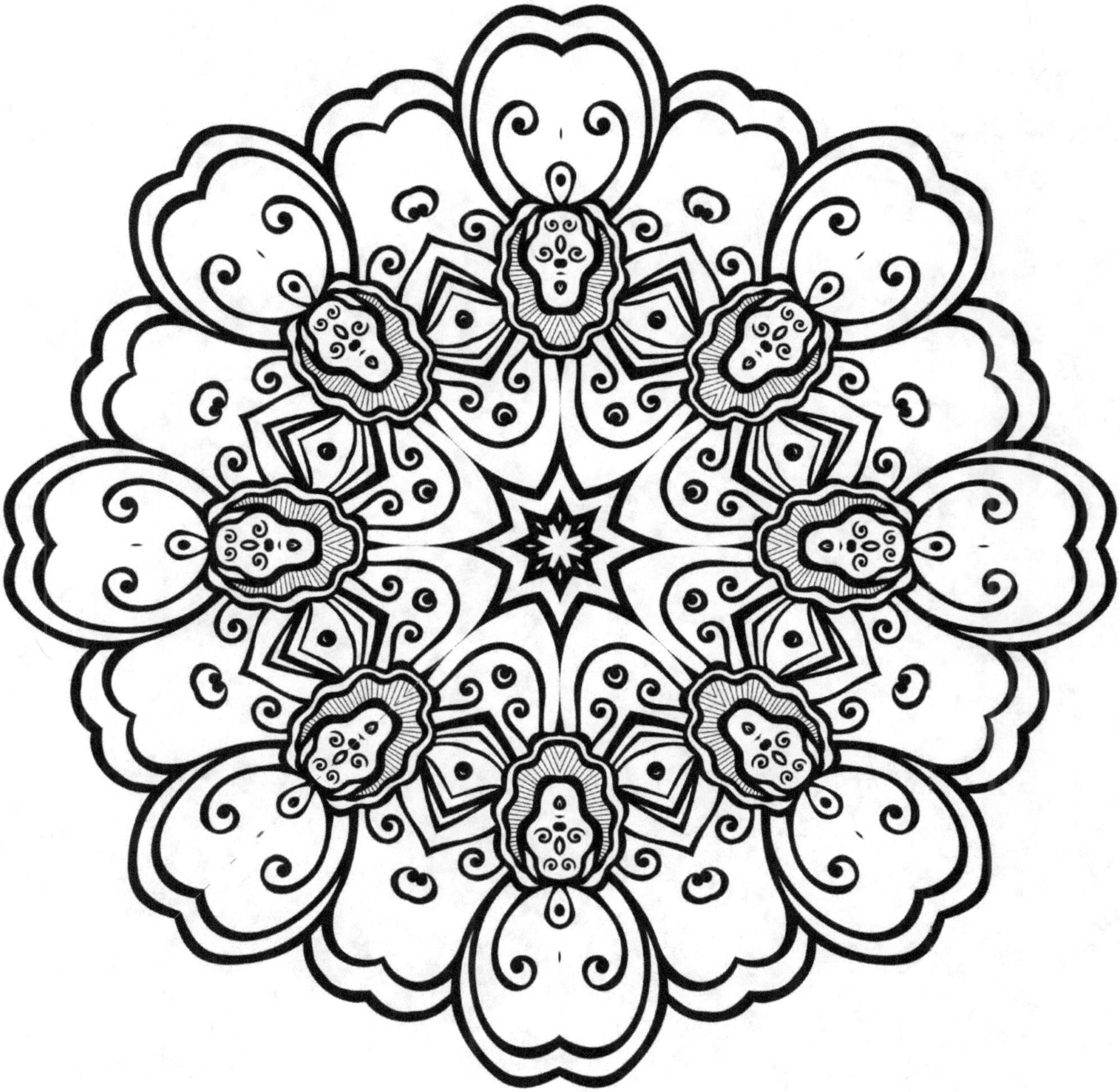

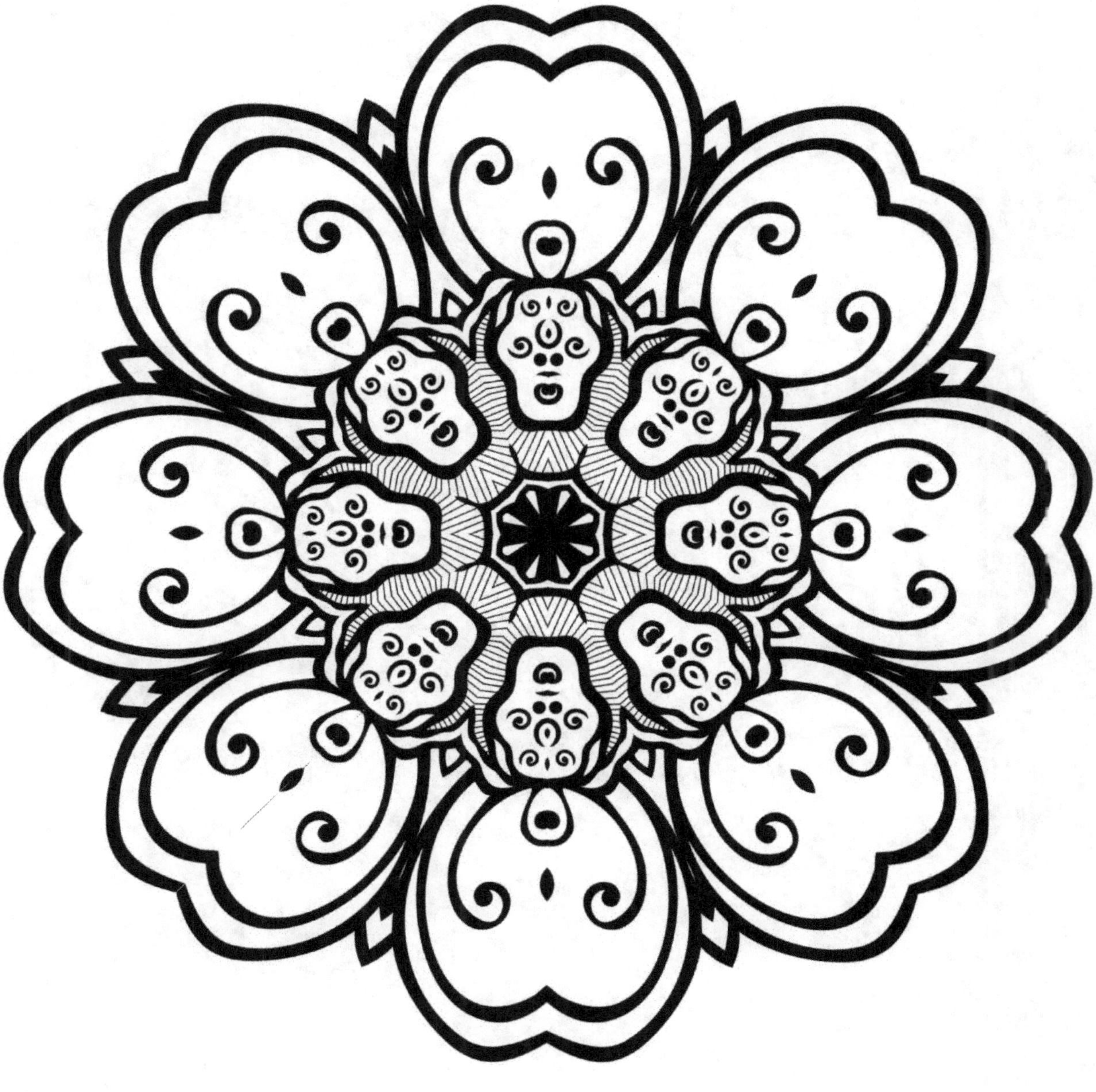

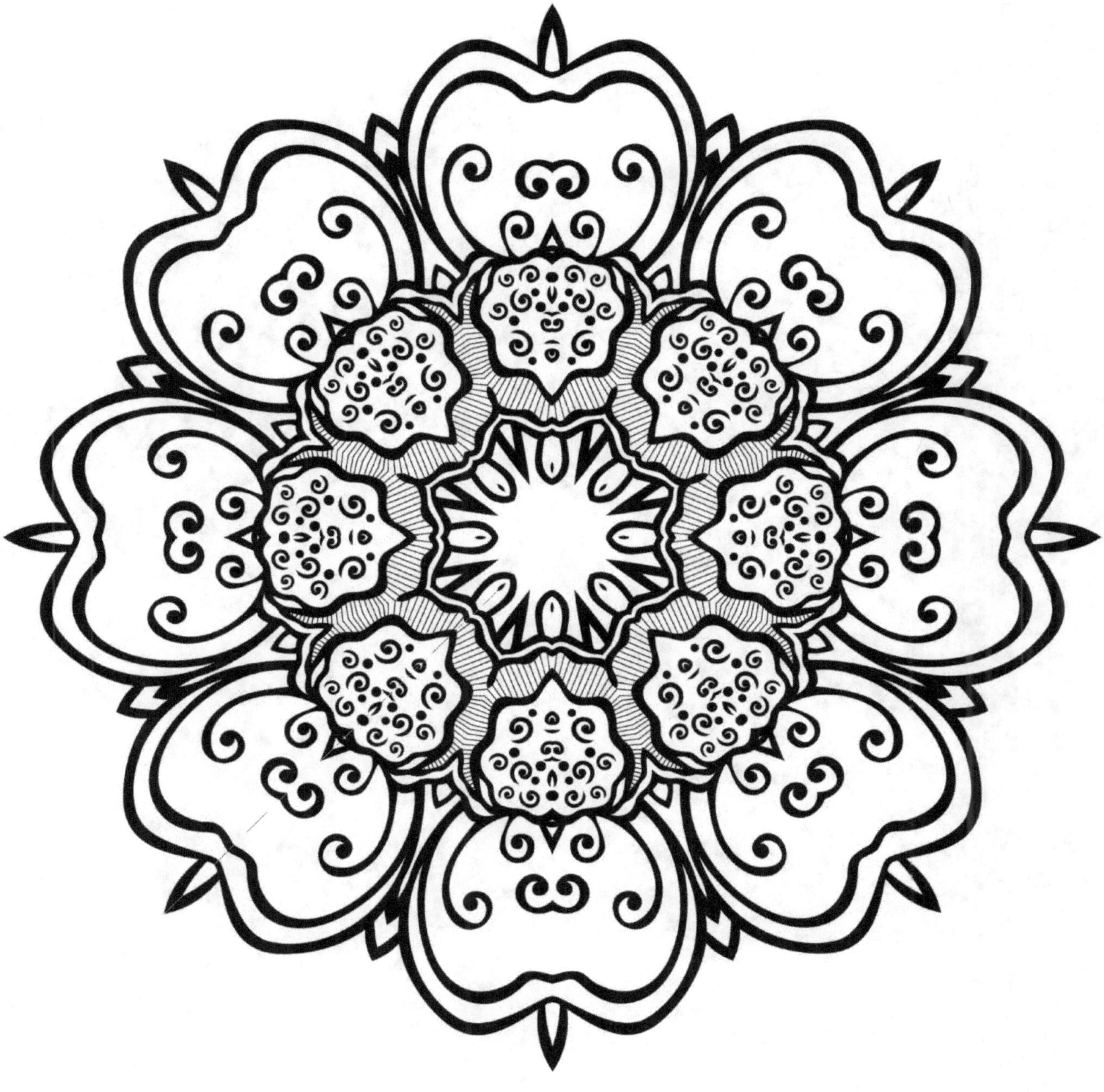

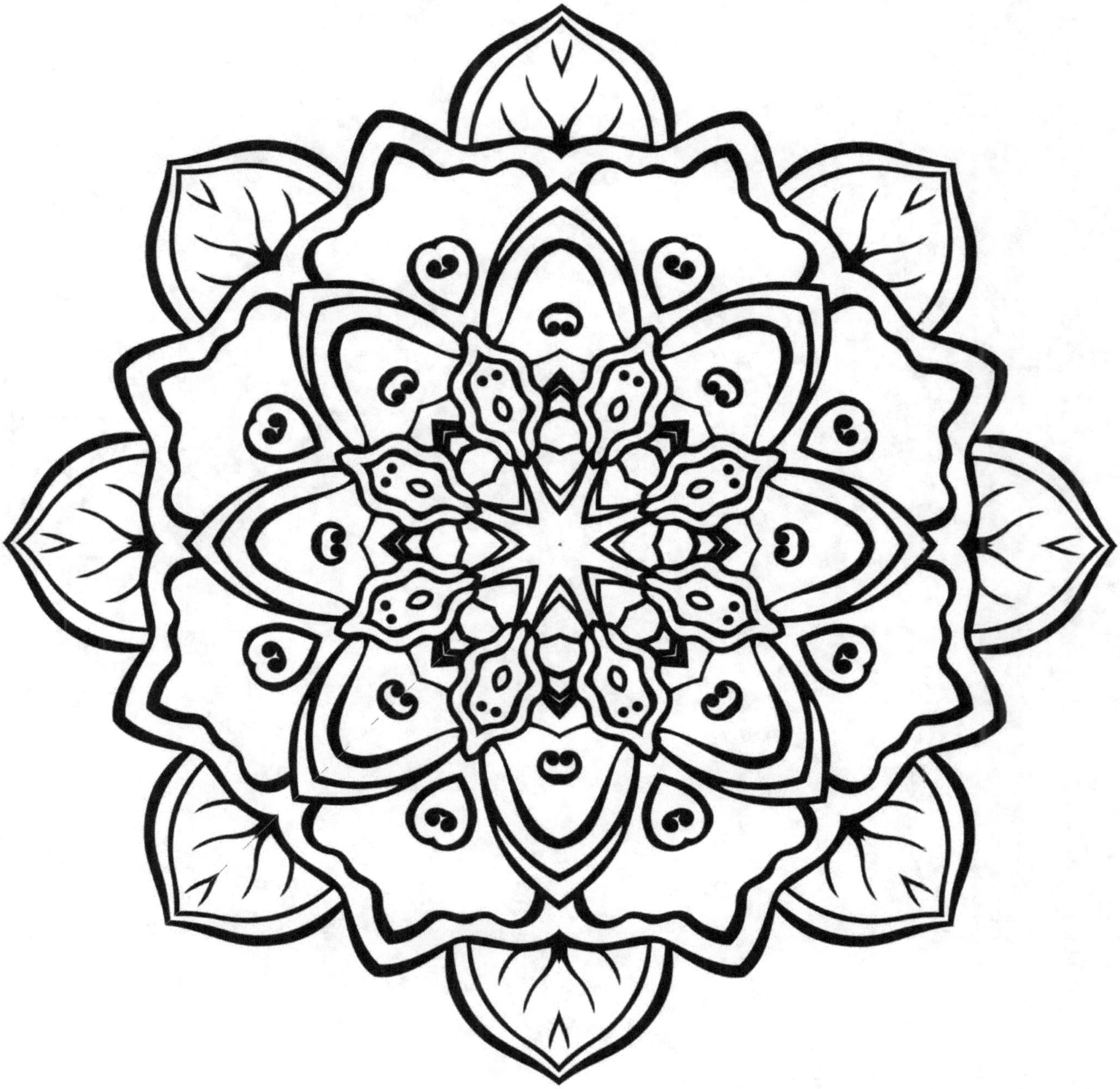

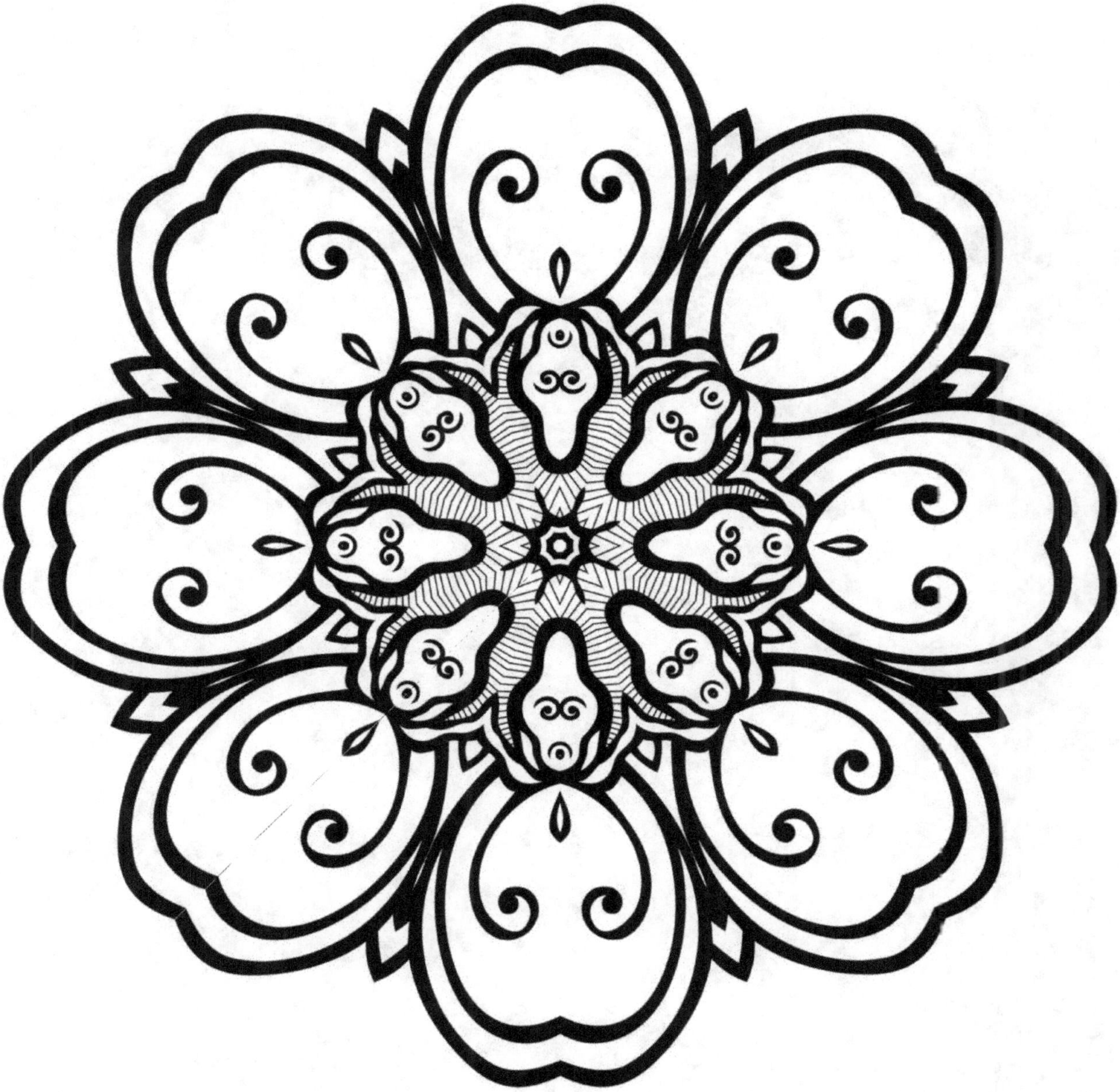

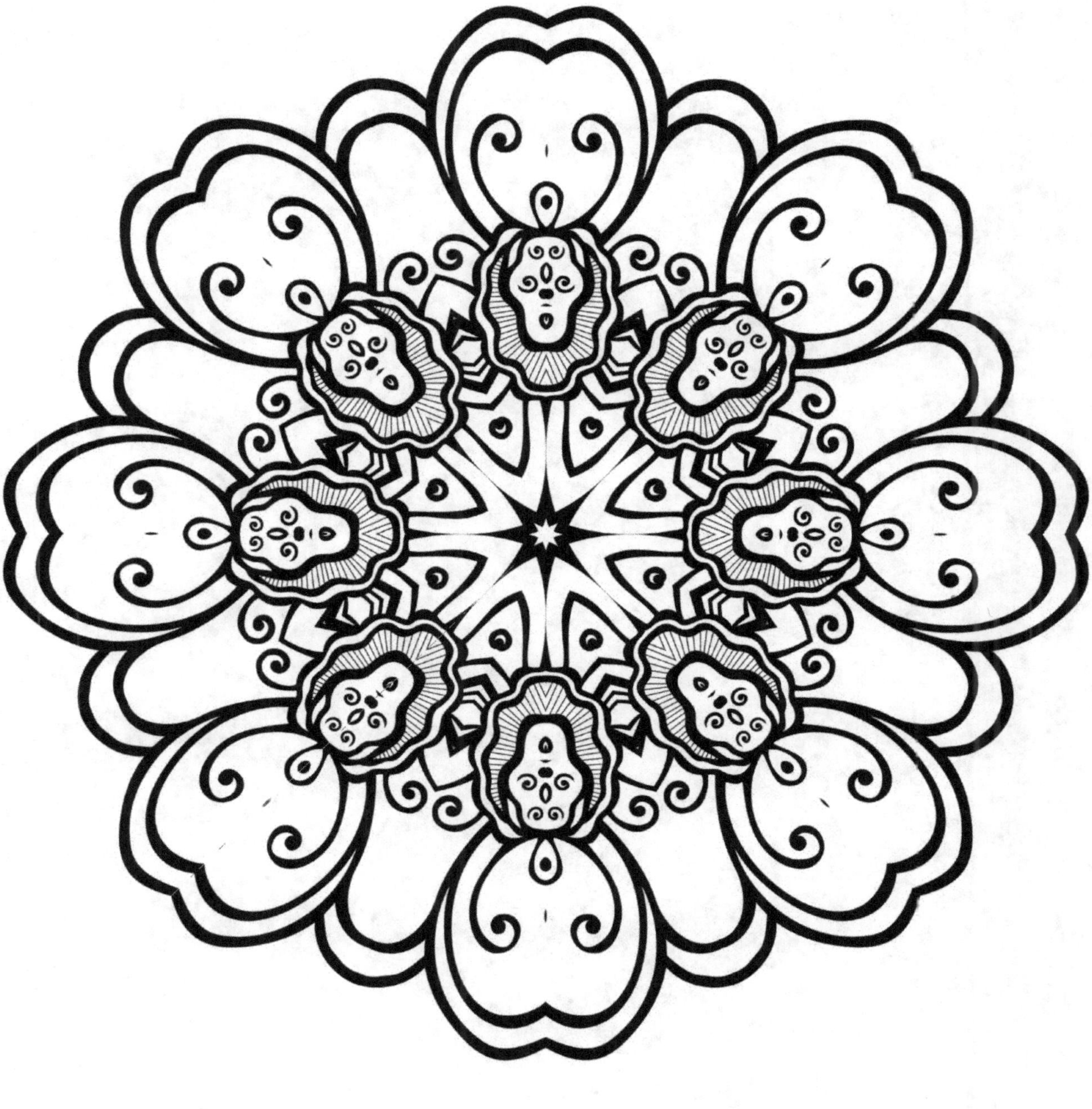

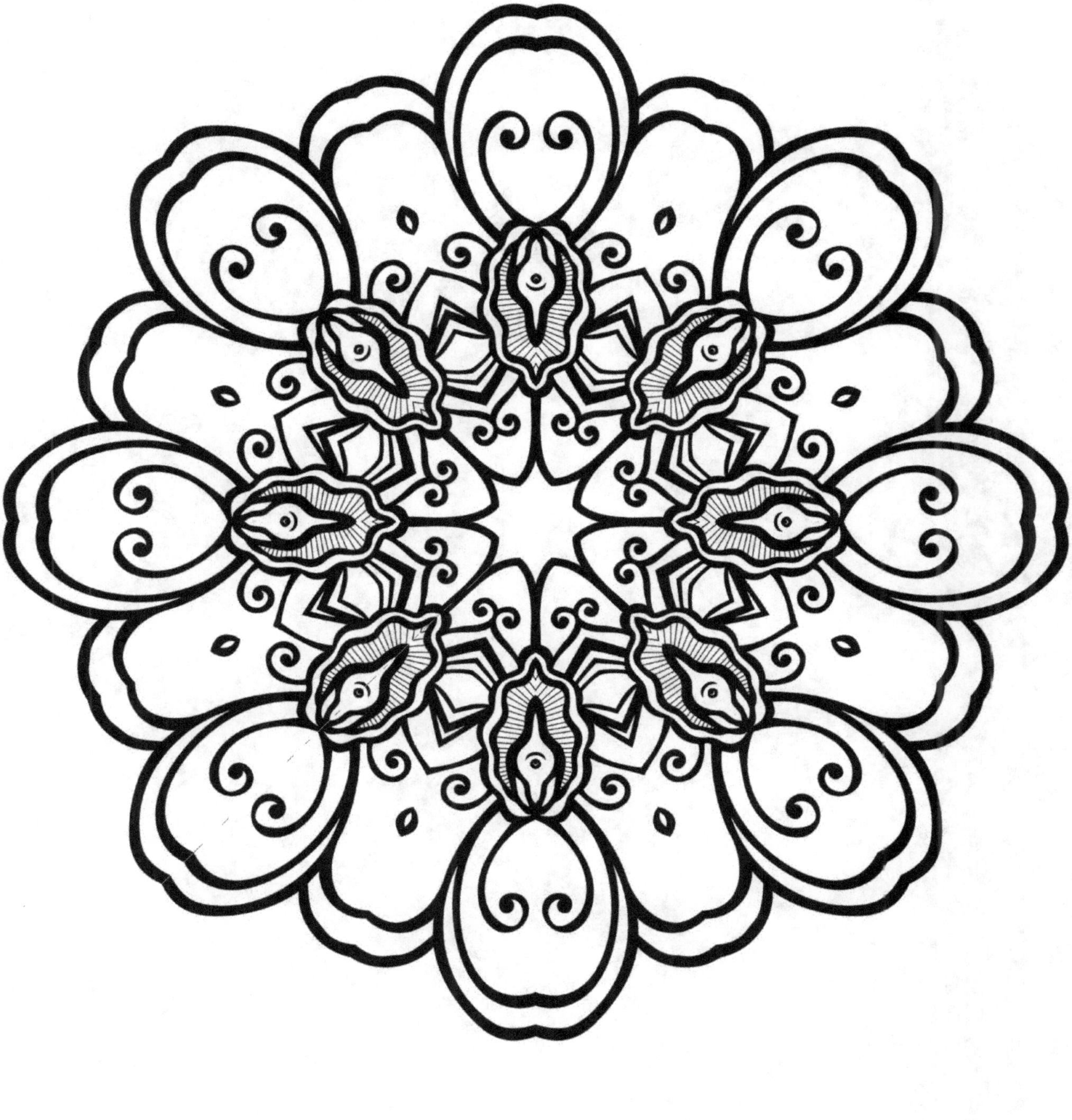

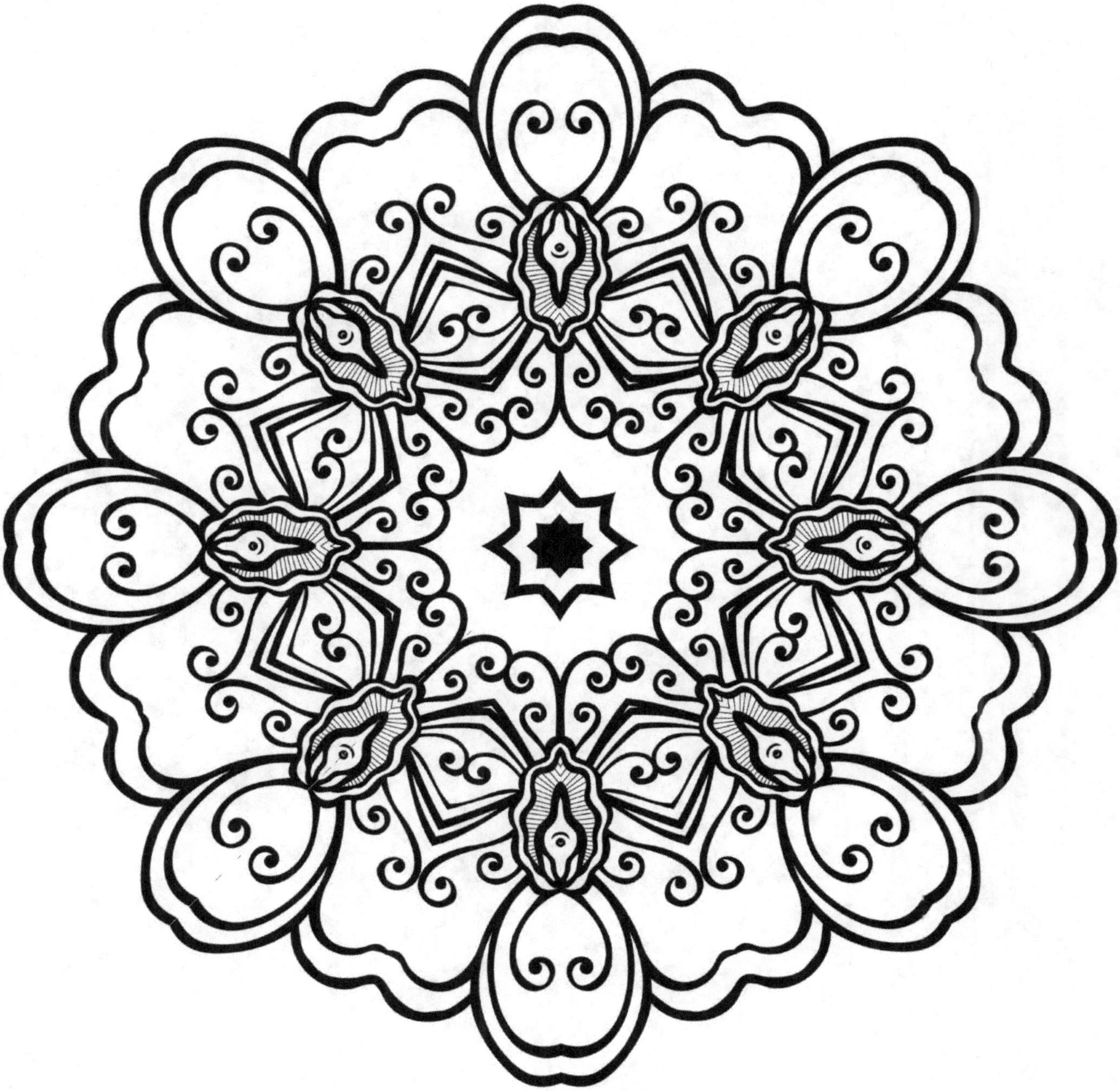

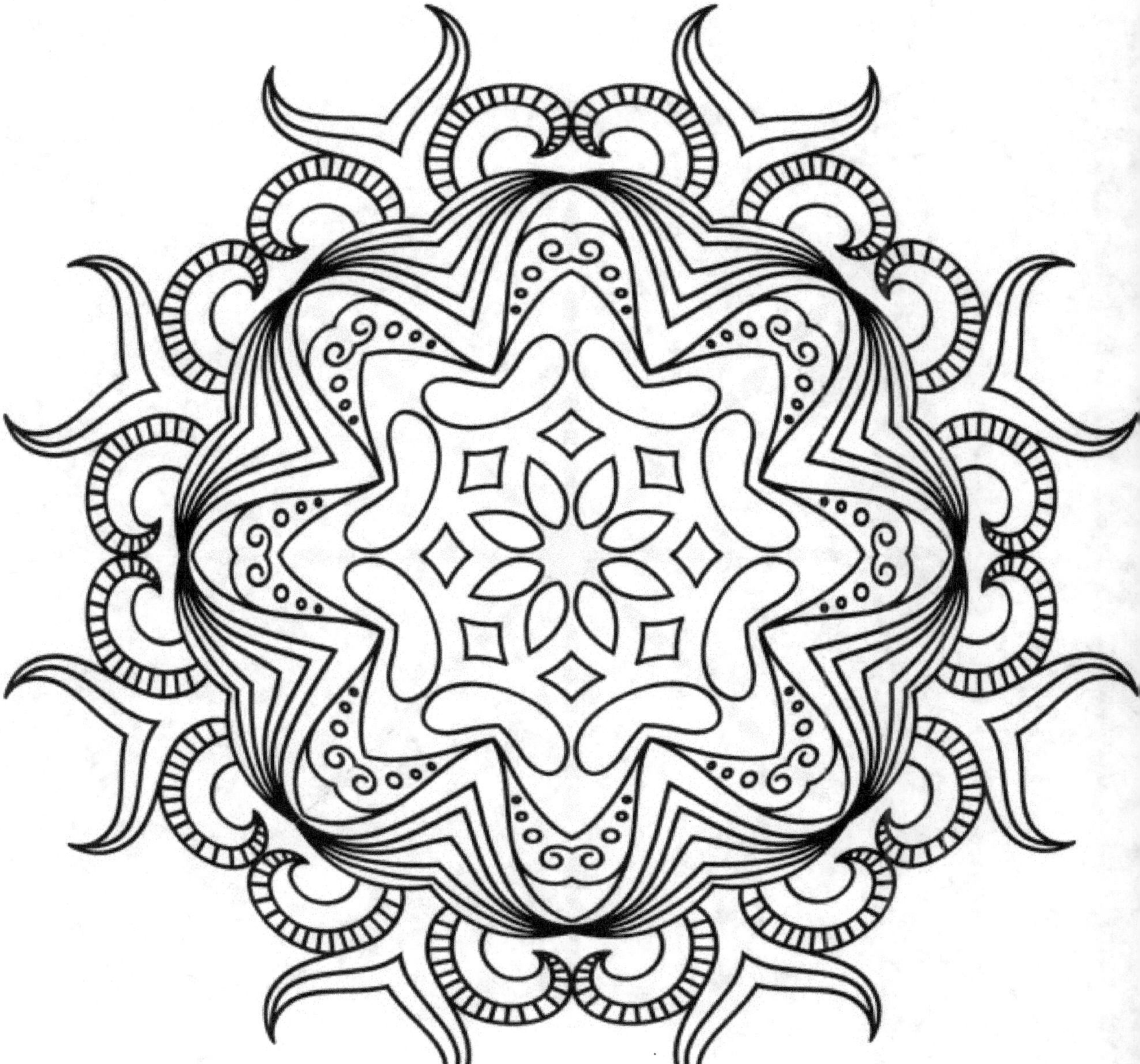

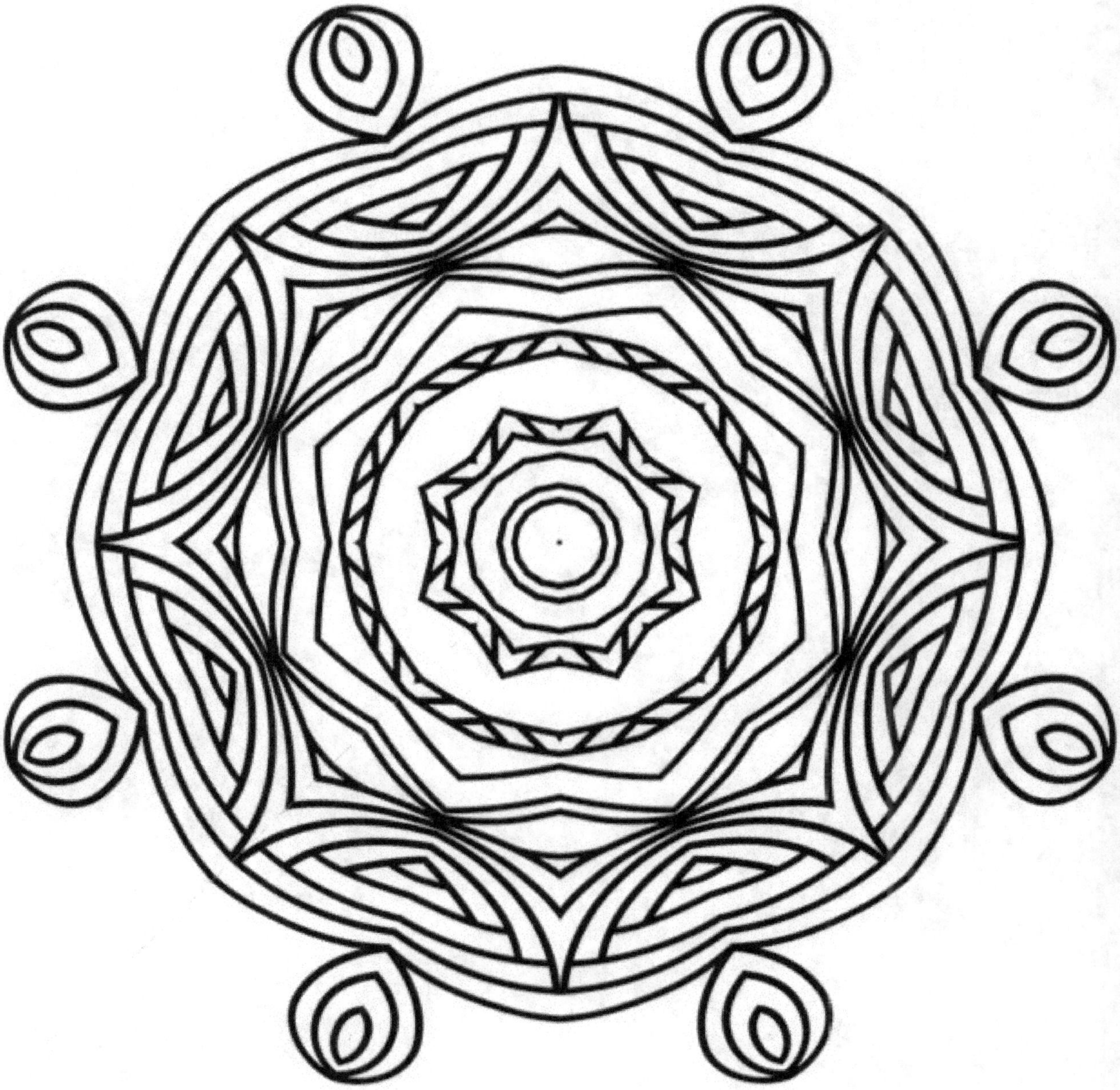

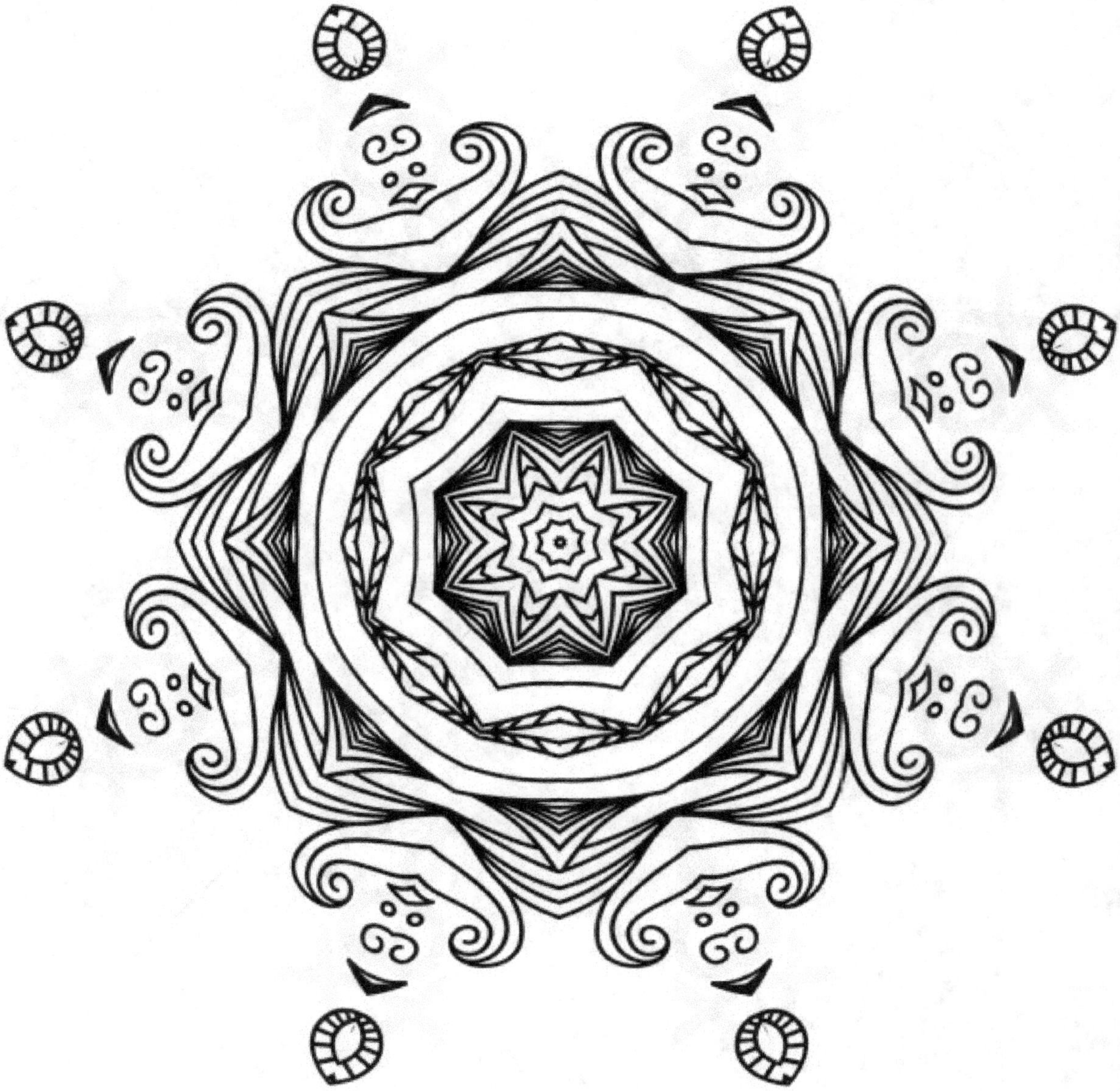

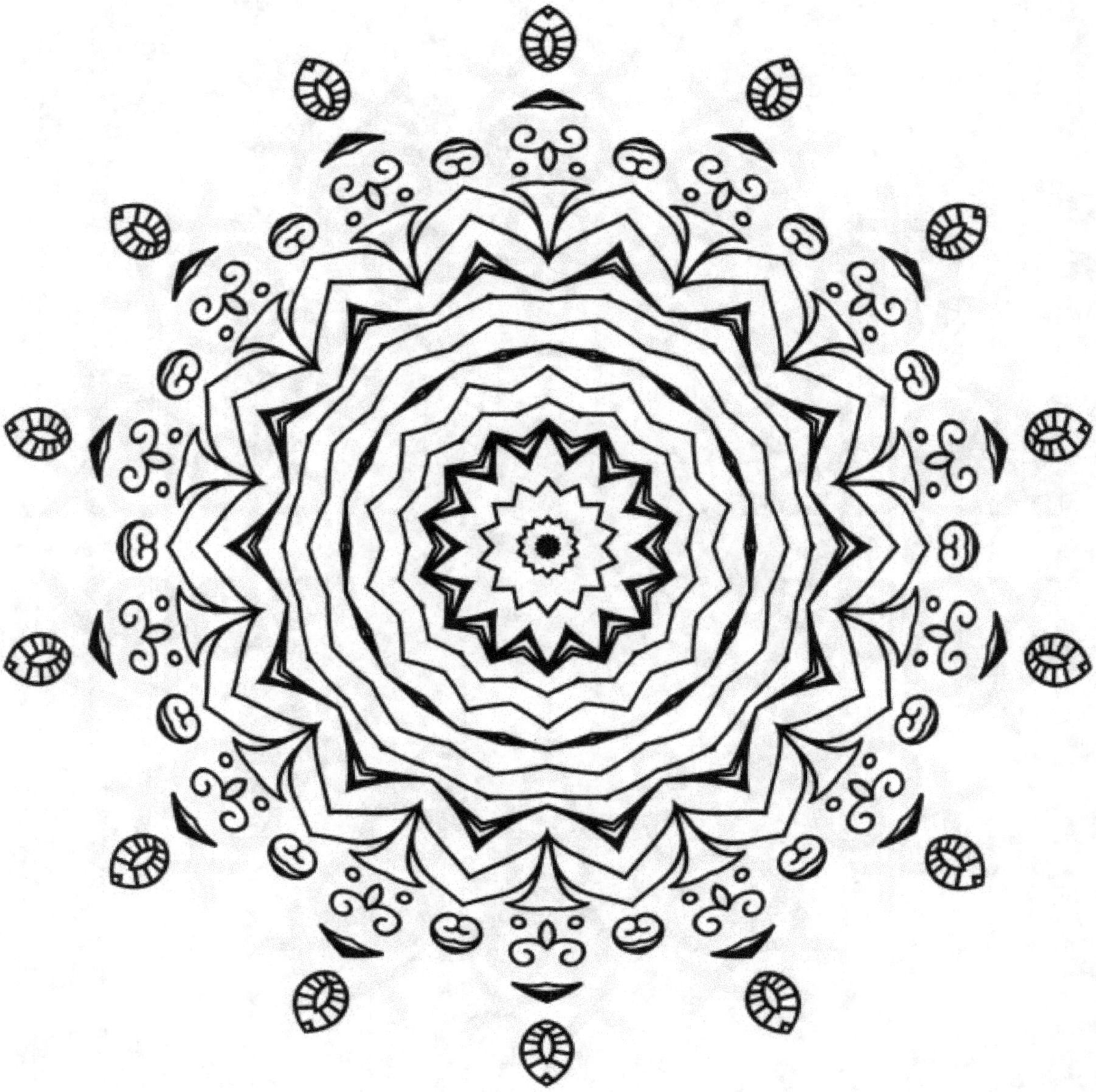

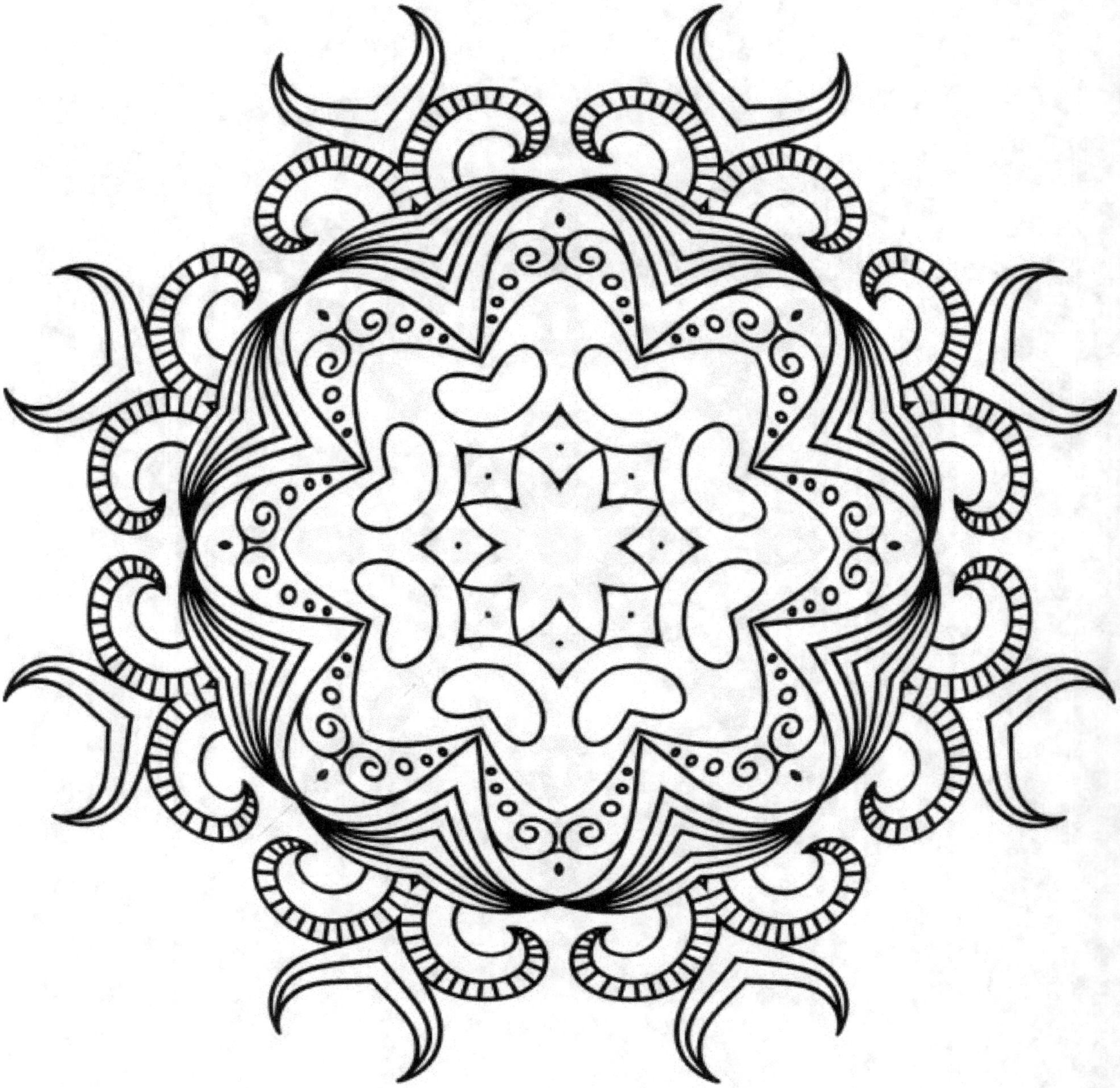

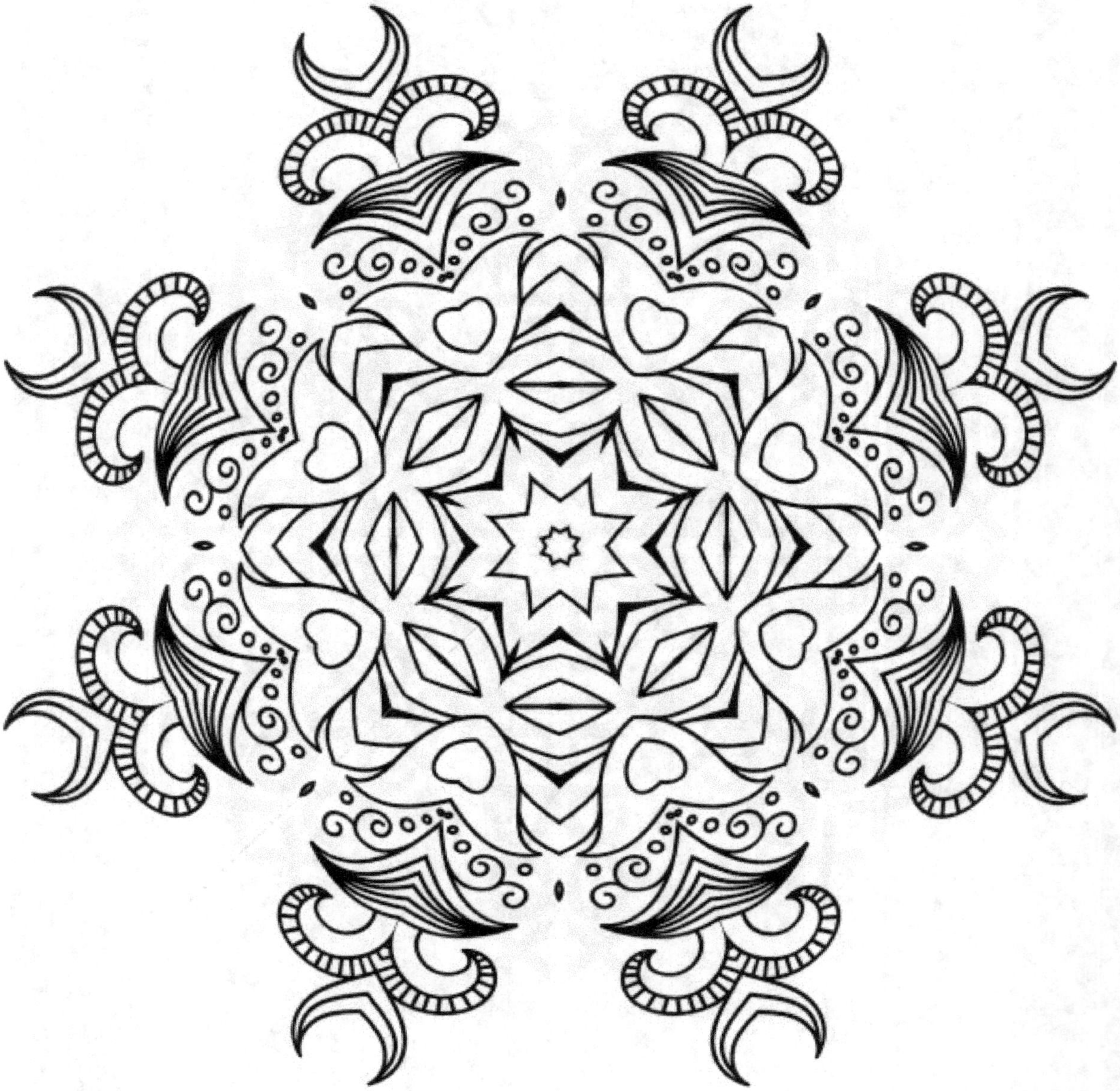

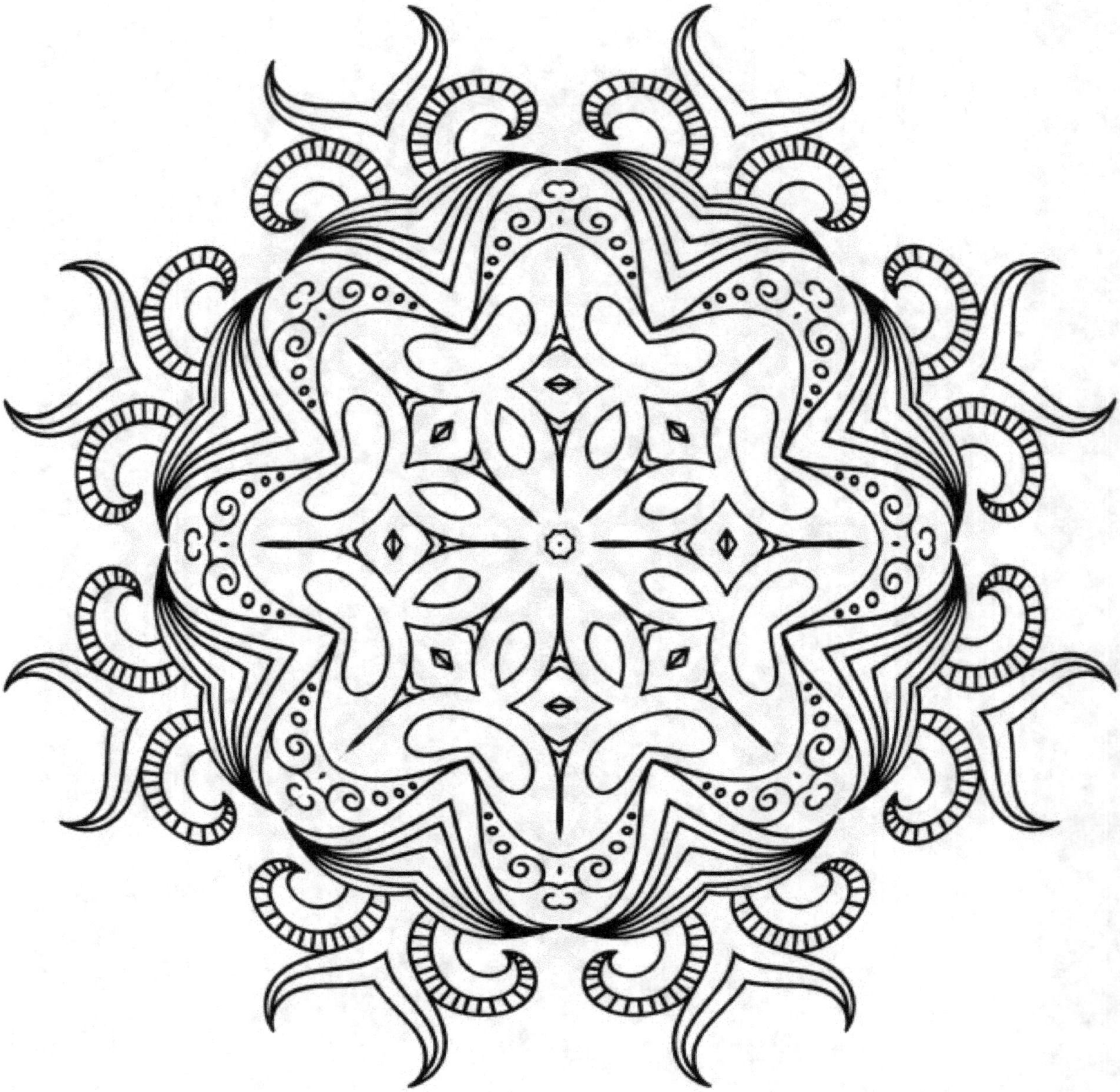

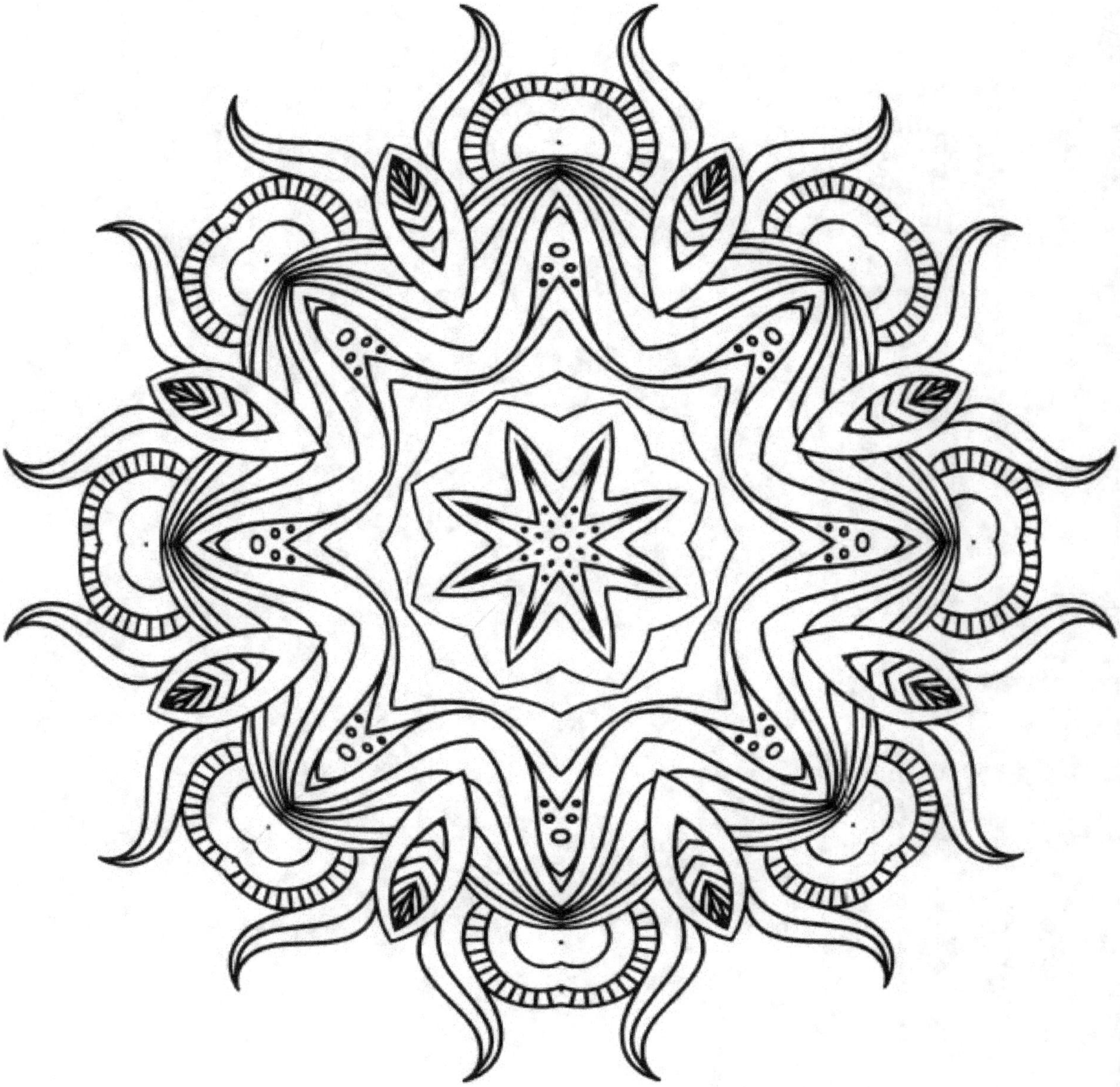

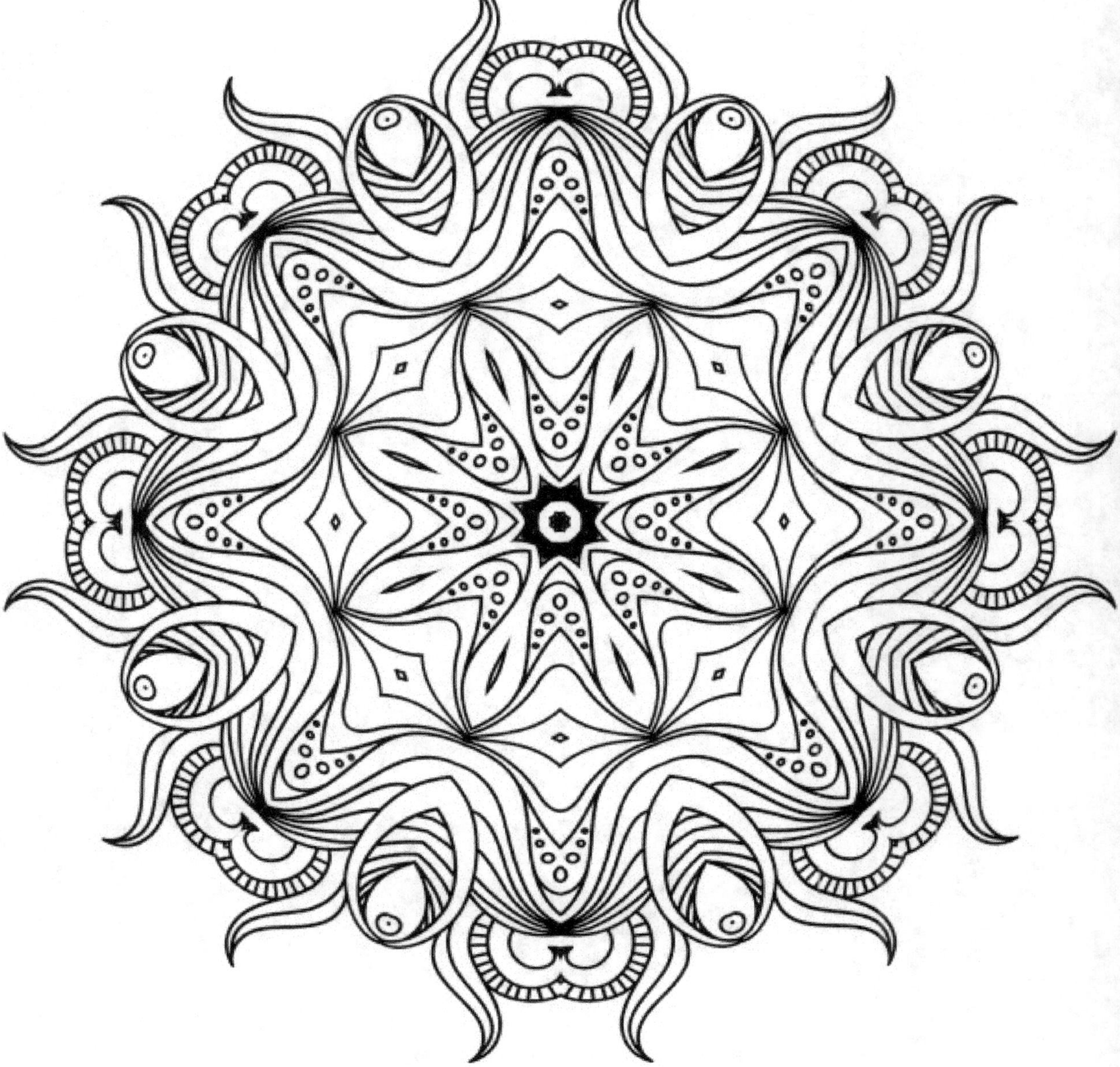

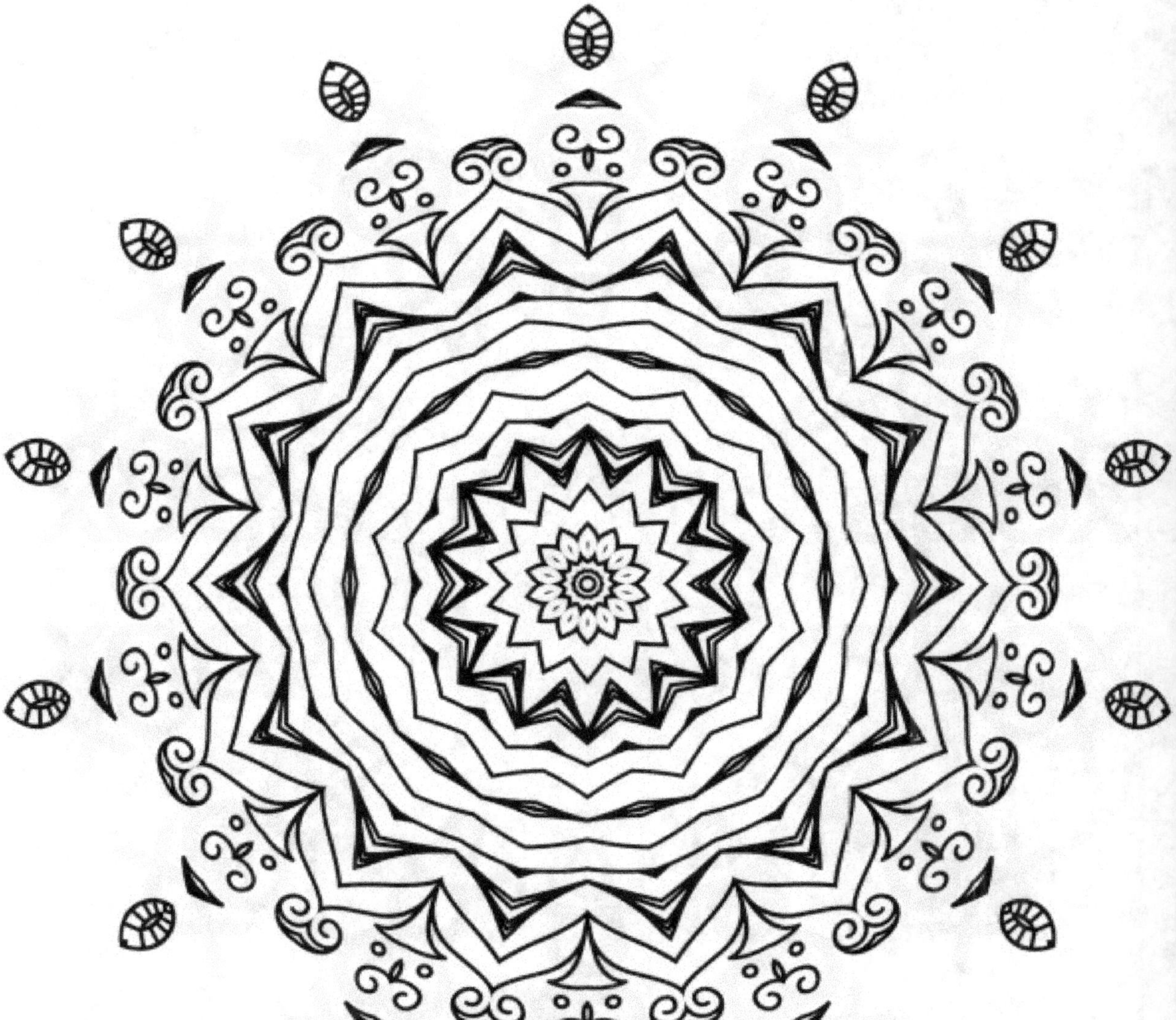

Hope you enjoy this coloring book.

Thank you.

www.ingramcontent.com/pod-product-compliance
Lightning Source LLC
Chambersburg PA
CBHW080832180526
45168CB00006B/2656
* 9 7 8 1 5 1 6 9 4 3 4 7 0 *